CE

# AN ESSAY
## ON THE
## PRINCIPLES OF HUMAN ACTION

# HISTORY OF PSYCHOLOGY SERIES

## GENERAL INTRODUCTION

The historically interesting works reprinted in this series helped to prepare the way for the science of psychology. Most of these books are long forgotten, but their relevance to the field is unmistakable. Many of the writings on mental and moral philosophy, published before the dawn of scientific procedures, have much to commend them to present-day scholars. These books serve as groundwork for a fuller account of the background from which the field emerged, and they should be attractive to students who seek in the past for hints of the future direction that certain types of research can take. Each work will have an Introduction stating the provenance and significance of the book and will add appropriate biographical information.

ROBERT I. WATSON
*General Editor*

*University of New Hampshire*

# AN ESSAY

## ON THE

## PRINCIPLES OF HUMAN ACTION

### AND

## Some Remarks On The Systems Of
## Hartley and Helvetius

(1805)

BY

## William Hazlitt

A FACSIMILE REPRODUCTION

WITH AN INTRODUCTION

BY

## John R. Nabholtz

GAINESVILLE, FLORIDA

## SCHOLARS' FACSIMILES & REPRINTS

1969

SCHOLARS' FACSIMILES & REPRINTS

1605 N.W. 14TH AVENUE

GAINESVILLE, FLORIDA, 32601, U.S.A.

HARRY R. WARFEL, GENERAL EDITOR


REPRODUCED FROM A COPY IN

AND WITH THE PERMISSION OF

ANDOVER-HARVARD
THEOLOGICAL LIBRARY


L.C. CATALOG CARD NUMBER: 70-75943

SBN 8201-1053-1


MANUFACTURED IN THE U.S.A.

# INTRODUCTION

*An Essay on the Principles of Human Action* was William Hazlitt's first published work, and to the end of his life he regarded it as his most important achievement. Its significance did not lie in its anticipation of any of the stylistic variety and power which were to inform such later masterpieces as *Lectures on the English Poets* (1818), *Table Talk* (1821-22), or *The Spirit of the Age* (1825); as the author himself admitted, the *Essay* is a "dry, tough, metaphysical *choke-pear.*"[1] Nor could Hazlitt have valued the work for its contemporary influence or reputation; its publication in 1805 drew little notice, and apart from Keats's enthusiastic reading of it in 1817 and a praiseful footnote-reference to it in Coleridge's *Lay Sermons* of the same year, it re-

---

[1] "Sir James Mackintosh" (1825), *The Complete Works of William Hazlitt,* ed. P. P. Howe, (London, 1930-34), XI, 102. With the exception of *An Essay on the Principles of Human Action,* all quotations from Hazlitt's writings are from Howe's edition.

mained virtually unknown during its author's lifetime. The *Essay* was important for its exposition of a "metaphysical discovery" concerning the creative and sympathetic powers of the mind, a "discovery" which Hazlitt saw as rescuing the mind from the chains of selfishness, sensation and habit in which it had been imprisoned by the "materialistic philosophy" of the eighteenth century. Modern students of English Romantic literature have recognized more and more the importance of the *Essay* as the seminal statement of Hazlitt's most cherished beliefs and the foundation for his later aesthetics and political writing. Its appearance in this Series will, it is hoped, make the work better known to students of British psychology and philosophy; for, whatever may be its relevance to the study of Romanticism, *An Essay on the Principles of Human Action* primarily defines itself in terms of the controversy which had raged in England since the time of Hobbes over the inherent selfishness or benevolence of human nature, and the possibility of grounding personal and social morality in the faculties and instincts of the mind.

The *Essay* had been in process of formulation for twelve years before its anonymous publication in 1805. In 1793, at the age of fifteen, Hazlitt had entered the Unitarian New College at Hackney to begin training for the ministry. Much to the disappointment of his father who was himself a Dissenting minister, Hazlitt quickly abandoned any interest in the ministry, and instead devoted himself to an intensive study of modern philosophy. During his stay at Hackney (1793-1795/96) and in the immediately succeeding years, Hazlitt read the leading British and French philosophers of the century, most notably Locke, Berkeley, Hartley, Priestley, Hume, Helvetius and d'Holbach. From the very beginning of his study, he found himself resisting the essentially selfish and mechanical picture of the mind described by philosophers in the tradition of Hobbes, and sought grounds for a refutation of their doctrines. As he recalls on pages 133-134 of the *Essay*,[2] it was while reading d'Holbach's *Système de la Nature* that he made his important "metaphysical discovery" of the "disinterestedness"

---

[2] Unaccountably, Hazlitt designated "Mirabeau" as the author of *Système de la Nature*. Still more unaccountable is the fact that he let this error stand in his dialogue-essays of 1828, "Self-Love and Benevolence," in which he quoted the relevant passage from the *Essay* of 1805.

of the mind and proceeded to write his analysis and refutation of "materialistic philosophy." The labor was long and frustrating. He was to report later that he had been "in vain trying, year after year, to write a single Essay, nay, a single page or sentence."[3] In 1798 he met Coleridge and attempted to explain his "discovery," but with little success. Despite this failure, Hazlitt was sufficiently stimulated by his encounter with the "Metaphysician-Bard" to try once more to complete the formal exposition of his argument: "I sat down to the task shortly afterwards for the twentieth time, got new pens and paper, determined to make clear work of it, wrote a few meagre sentences in the skeleton-style of a mathematical demonstration, stopped halfway down the second page; and, after trying in vain to pump up any words, images, notions, apprehensions, facts, or observations, from that gulph of abstraction in which I had plunged myself for four or five years preceding, gave up the attempt as labour in vain, and shed tears of helpless despondency on the blank unfinished paper."[4]

---

[3] "On Reading Old Books" (1821), *Works,* XII, 229.

[4] "My First Acquaintance with Poets" (1823), *Works,* XVII, 114.

With this renewed failure, Hazlitt apparently gave up all thoughts of writing, and began the study of painting under the guidance of his brother John Hazlitt, a London portrait painter. The succeeding years were devoted to the profession of painting, including a visit to the Louvre in 1802 to make copies of the masterpieces there, and a notorious visit to the Lake District in 1803 to paint the portraits of Coleridge, Wordsworth, and their children. In 1804 he returned to his writing and brought the *Essay* to completion.

Although he had early abandoned any formal commitment to his religious heritage, Hazlitt always retained the mind and character of a Dissenter; a vigorous opponent of established authority, he assailed those habits and prejudices which inhibit the development of individual personality and belief. The *Essay* of 1805 speaks to this prevailing bias in Hazlitt. It is a strenuous attack on modern philosophy for its representation of man as limited to the impulses of past or present sensation, forever wedded to his own concern, and incapable of creative operations upon his experience or generous impulses toward others.

Hazlitt bases his argument for "disinterested benevolence" on three faculties of the mind: memory, consciousness, and imagination, which concern themselves respectively with events of the past, present, and future. Hazlitt agrees with his opponents that in regard to past and present, man is a creature of self-concern, the subject of sensations which act in mechanical ways; and that personal identity is established in these terms. However, future events, *by the very fact that they are future,* cannot be known by immediate sensation; our relation to them cannot, therefore, be established in terms of mechanical self-interest or exclusive personal identity. The future exists as an idea of the *imagination,* that faculty which creates and projects objects of future good or evil. These ideas of the imagination call out in us corresponding desires for, or aversion to, the good or evil projected. The central point of Hazlitt's "discovery" is that it is the good or evil which provokes in us feelings of desire or aversion, not our sense of self-interest. Objects "are not converted into good and evil," he argues, "by being impressed on our minds, but they affect our minds in a certain manner because they are essentially good or evil" (p. 52). There must be some object of good, or there would be no feelings of desire aroused, and no motive for action. If love of self were our exclusive principle of operation, we would remain forever fixed, robot-like, on our past and present sensations.

In Hazlitt's dialectic the love of self does not precede, but follows from, the knowledge of the good; we silently transfer our love of the good and our happiness in the experience of it to ourselves as the persons benefited by it. However, precisely because it is the good which draws us and not self-interest, as we become aware of the good existing for and benefiting others, the same feelings of happiness will be aroused at another's possession of the good and the same transfer of love from the object to the person will occur. In these terms, Hazlitt may argue: "The imagination, by means of which alone I can anticipate future objects, or be interested in them, must carry me out of myself into the feelings of others by one and the same process by which I am thrown forward as it were into my future being, and interested in it. I could not love myself, if I were not capable of loving others. Self-love, used in this sense, is in it's [*sic*] fundamental principle the same with disinterested benevolence" (p. 3).

The central target of Hazlitt's argument for the sympathetic imagination as the instru-

ment of moral action is the Hobbesian conception of the mind as a *mechanism* governed
by inevitable and irreversible laws of self-interest. Just as Wordsworth and Coleridge rejected as antithetical to true religious feeling
the Deistic conception of the universe as a
well-ordered machine, so too Hazlitt rejected
the mechanical conception of the mind as
subversive of man's distinction as a moral
being. A second strain in modern philosophy
which supported mechanism was the Theory
of Association set forth in David Hartley's
*Observations on Man* (1749).[5] In the con-
cluding section of the *Essay*, Hazlitt provides
an extended refutation of Hartley's theory, a
refutation following from the same view of
the mind as creative, dynamic, and sympathetic advanced earlier in the work. Hazlitt
agrees that association, that is, the connection
of different local impressions on material
points within the brain corresponding to the
order of the sensory experience, is one mode
of mental life; but it cannot be the exclusive
or primary one. If all mental life consists in
the mere juxtaposition of impressions in the
brain in the order of time and place in which

---

[5] A facsimile reproduction of Hartley's work was
issued by Scholars' Facsimiles & Reprints in 1966.

they originally occurred, then man would be incapable of defining and evaluating the relationship between these impressions, or of bringing together the impressions of different senses, or of discovering communication between present and past experience, or of constructing classes of experience. Against Hartley's explanation of mental action, Hazlitt argues that the mind is not the mere repository of temporally and spatially related sensations, but is an independent power "modifying and reacting upon all the ideas contained in it." The mind relates the "manifold" objects of sensation in terms of uniquely human values and goals, and directs the will by this evaluation and synthesis of experience, not by the accidental order of experience itself. In answering Hartley's associationism as well as Helvetius' theory of self-interest, Hazlitt rests his case on man as master of his experience, not its passive victim.

Hazlitt's argument for the creative and sympathetic powers of the mind, so strenuously set forth in the *Essay* of 1805, was to inform virtually everything he wrote until his death twenty-five years later. The major premise of his aesthetics and literary criticism was the artist's ability to move beyond his own limited identity into sympathetic union with the object of his contemplation. In these terms, Hazlitt was to praise Shakespeare's Protean ability "only to think of any thing in order to become that thing, with all the circumstances belonging to it";[6] and to criticize contemporary poets, Wordsworth and Byron most notably, for their self-centered aversion to "outward fact." His political writings were directed against those dogmas and institutions which rivet man to his economic and social environment and thus inhibit the flowering of individual consciousness and sympathetic union between classes, nations, and races. His famous personal essays, such as "On Going a Journey" and "A Farewell to Essay-Writing," are brilliant demonstrations of the imaginative ordering of memories and present sensations in terms of both personal and broadly human aspirations.

In 1826 Hazlitt had declared that "the only pretension, of which I am tenacious, is that of being a metaphysician."[7] *An Essay on the Principles of Human Action* was the basis for that "pretension," and it is the essential document for understanding and evalu-

---

[6] "On Shakespeare and Milton" (1818), *Works*, V, 48.

[7] "On Envy (A Dialogue)," *Works*, XII, 98.

ating William Hazlitt's place in the intellectual and literary history of his time.

John R. Nabholtz
*University of Rochester*
*Rochester, New York*
*May 25, 1968*

# AN ESSAY

## ON THE

# PRINCIPLES OF HUMAN ACTION:

BEING AN ARGUMENT IN FAVOUR OF
THE NATURAL DISINTERESTEDNESS
OF THE HUMAN MIND.

TO WHICH ARE ADDED,

SOME REMARKS ON THE SYSTEMS OF

HARTLEY AND HELVETIUS.

LONDON:

PRINTED FOR J. JOHNSON, NO. 72, ST. PAUL'S
CHURCH-YARD.

1805.

Printed by E. Hemsted, Great New-Street,
Fetter-Lane.

# AN ARGUMENT

## IN DEFENCE OF THE

## NATURAL DISINTERESTEDNESS
## OF THE HUMAN MIND.

IT is the design of the following Essay
to shew that the human mind is naturally
disinterested, or that it is naturally interested in the welfare of others in the same
way, and from the same direct motives, by
which we are impelled to the pursuit of
our own interest.

The objects in which the mind is interested may be either past or present, or
future. These last alone can be the objects of rational or voluntary pursuit; for
neither the past, nor present can be altered for the better, or worse by any efforts of the will. It is only from the in-

B

terest excited in him by future objects that
man becomes a moral agent, or is deno-
minated selfish, or the contrary, according
to the manner in which he is affected by
what relates to his own *future* interest, or
that of others. I propose then to shew
that the mind is naturally interested in it's
own welfare in a peculiar mechanical manner, only as far as relates to it's past, or
present impressions. I have an interest in
my own actual feelings or impressions by
means of consciousness, and in my past
feelings by means of memory, which I
cannot have in the past, or present feelings
of others, because these faculties can only
be exerted upon those things which immediately and properly affect myself. As
an affair of sensation, or memory, I can
feel no interest in any thing but what relates to myself in the strictest sense. But
this distinction does not apply to future
objects, or to those impressions, which
determine my voluntary actions. I have
not the same sort of exclusive, or mecha-

not the same sort of exclusive, or mechanical self-interest in my future being or
welfare, because I have no distinct faculty
giving me a direct present interest in my
future sensations, and none at all in those
of others. The imagination, by means
of which alone I can anticipate future objects, or be interested in them, must carry
me out of myself into the feelings of others
by one and the same process by which I
am thrown forward as it were into my
future being, and interested in it. I could
not love myself, if I were not capable of
loving others. Self-love, used in this
sense, is in it's fundamental principle the
same with disinterested benevolence.

Those who have maintained the doctrine of the natural selfishness of the human mind have always taken it for granted as a self-evident principle that *a man
must love himself*, or that it is not less
absurd to ask why a man should be interested in his own personal welfare, than
it would be to ask why a man in a

state of actual enjoyment, or suffering likes what gives him pleasure, and dislikes what gives him pain. They say, that no such necessity, nor any positive reason whatever can be conceived to exist for my promoting the welfare of another, since I cannot possibly feel the pleasures, or pains which another feels without first becoming that other, that our interests must be as necessarily distinct as we ourselves are, that the good which I do to another, in itself and for it's own sake can be nothing to me. *Good* is a term relative only to the being who enjoys it. The good which he does not feel must be matter of perfect indifference to him. How can I be required to make a painful exertion, or sacrifice a present convenience to serve another, if I am to be nothing the better for it? I waste my powers out of myself without sharing in the effects which they produce. Whereas when I sacrifice my present ease or convenience, for the sake of a greater good to myself at

a future period, the same being who
suffers afterwards enjoys, both the loss
and the gain are mine, I am upon the
whole a gainer in real enjoyment, and
am therefore justified to myself: I act
with a view to an end in which I have
a real, substantial interest. The human
soul, continue some of these writers, naturally thirsts after happiness; it either
enjoys, or seeks to enjoy. It constantly
reaches forward towards the possession of
happiness, it strives to draw it to itself,
and to be absorbed in it. But as the
mind cannot enjoy any good but what it
possesses within itself, neither can it seek
to produce any good but what it can enjoy: it is just as idle to suppose that the
love of happiness or good should prompt
any being to give up his own interest for
the sake of another, as it would be to attempt to allay violent thirst by giving water
to another to drink.

Now I can conceive that a man must
be necessarily interested in his own actual

feelings, whatever these may be, merely because he feels them. He cannot
help receiving pain from what gives him
pain, or pleasure from what gives him
pleasure. But I cannot conceive how
he can have the same necessary, absolute
interest in whatever relates to himself, or
in his own pleasures and pains, generally speaking, whether he feels them, or
not. This kind of reasoning, which in itself is all along founded in a mere play of
words, could not have gained the assent
of thinking men but for the force with
which the idea of self habitually clings to
the mind of every man, binding it as
with a spell, deadening it's discriminating
powers, and spreading the confused associations which belong only to past and
present impressions over the whole of our
imaginary existence. It therefore becomes difficult to separate ideas which
have been thus knit together by custom,
or "by a long tract of time, by the use
of language, and want of reflection."

If it were possible for a man's particular successive interests to be all bound up in one general feeling of self-interest as they are all comprehended under the same word, *self*, or if a man on the rack really felt no more than he must have done from the apprehension of the same punishment a year before, there would be some foundation for this reasoning, which supposes the mind to have the same absolute interest in it's own feelings both past, present, and to come. I say the sophism here employed consists in comparing the motives by which we are interested in the welfare of others with the mechanical impulses of self-love, as if because we are mechanically affected by the actual impression of objects on our senses in a manner in which we cannot be affected by the feelings of others, all our feelings with respect to ourselves must be of the same kind, and we could feel no interest in any thing but what was excited in the same way. It is plain we are not interested in our general, remote welfare in the same manner, or by the same necessity that we are affected by the actual sense of pleasure, or pain. We have no instinctive secret sympathy with our future sensations by which we are attracted either consciously or unconsciously to our greatest good; we are for the most part indifferent to it, ignorant of it. We certainly do not know, and we very often care as little what is to happen to ourselves in future: it has no more effect upon us in any way, than if it were never to happen. Were it not for this shortsightedness, and insensibility, where would be the use, or what would become of the rules of personal prudence?

It will be said, I know, that this is foreign to the purpose; for that whether he feels it, or not, every man *has* a real interest in his own welfare which he cannot have in that of another person. First, this is to shift the ground of the argument; for it requires to be made out how a man can be said to have an interest in what he does not feel. There is not evidently the same contradiction in supposing him not to be particularly interested in feelings which he has not, as there is in supposing him not to be interested in his actual, sensible pleasures and pains. Secondly, I shall very readily grant that *to have* and *to feel* an interest in any thing are not always convertible terms, that is, an interest may attach or belong to an individual in some way or other though he does not feel it at the time. My having a *real* interest in any object may refer to the matter of fact that such an object will some time or other exist: now the reality of it's existence does not certainly depend on my feeling an interest in it previously. Neither is the reality of another's pleasures, or pains affected by my not feeling such an interest in them as I ought to do. The feelings of others are evidently as real, or as much matters of fact in themselves as my own feelings can ever be. This distinction between that which is true and what has merely an imaginary existence, or none at all, does not therefore so far apply to the question, if by a real interest be meant that which relates to a real object, for it is supposed at first that this object does not excite any immediate or real interest in the mind. Another difference that may be insisted on is this, that I *shall have* a real sensible interest in my own future feelings which I cannot possibly have in those of others. I must therefore as the same individual have the same necessary interest in them at present. This may either proceed on the supposition of the absolute, metaphysical identity of my individual being, so that whatever can be affirmed of that principle at any time must be strictly and logically true of it at all times, which is a wild and absurd notion; or it may refer to some other less strict connection between my present and future self, in consequence of which I am considered as the same being, the different events and impressions of my life constituting one regular succession of conscious feelings. In this sense, the saying that *I have* a general interest in whatever concerns my future welfare in fact amounts to no more than affirming, that *I shall have* an interest in that welfare, or that I am nominally and in certain other respects the same being who will hereafter have a real interest in it. The reason why we are so ready to attribute a real identity of interests to the same person is, that we have an indistinct idea of extended consciousness, and a community of feelings as essential to the same thinking being; so that whatever interests me at one time must interest me, or be capable of interesting me, at other times. Now this continued consciousness only serves to connect my past with my present impressions. It only acts retrospectively. I have not previously the same sympathy with my future being that I have with my past being, nor consequently the same natural or necessary interest in my future welfare that I have in my past. Lastly, it may be said, that there is something in the very *idea* of pleasure or pain as affecting myself which naturally excites a lively, unavoidable interest in my mind. I cannot conceive how the mere idea of self can produce any such effect as is here described, unless we imagine that self-love literally consists in the love of self, or in a proper attachment to our own persons instead of referring to the feelings of desire and aversion, hope, and fear, &c. excited in us by those things which either do, or may immediately affect ourselves. In consequence of the impression of many such objects on the thinking being, we shall come no doubt to connect a sense of self-interest with this very being, with the motions of our blood, and with life itself, and shall by degrees transfer the emotions of interest excited by particular positive feelings to the idea of our own interest generally speaking. This however must be the work of time, the gradual result of habit, and reflection, and cannot be the natural reason why a man pursues his own welfare, or is interested in his own feelings. I think therefore that in the first instance the idea of personal pleasure or pain can only affect the mind as a distinct idea of that which is in itself the object of desire, or aversion, and that the idea of self is nothing more than the first and most distinct idea we have of a being capable of receiving pleasure and pain. It will be the business of the greatest part of the following essay to make out these several points more distinctly.

There is another hypothesis which I shall just mention, that holds a sort of middle place between the two opposite ones already stated. The partisans of this more liberal philosophy, who could not suppress the consciousness of humane and benevolent dispositions in themselves, or the proofs of them in others, but yet knew not how to reconcile these feelings with the supposed selfishness of human nature, have endeavoured to account for the different impulses of generous affection from habit, or the constant connection between the

pleasures and pains of others, and our own,
by which means we come at last to confound
our own interests with theirs, and to feel the
same anxiety for their welfare without any
view to our own advantage. A man according to this hypothesis becomes attached
to others as he becomes attached to any
other indifferent object, to a tree, or a stone,
from familiarity, and the frequent association of his immediate gratification with the
indifferent idea; and this attachment once
formed, he must afterwards be interested
in their welfare whether he will or no.
An example of this may be given in boys
at school. A boy is confined to his task
at the same time with his school-fellows;
he feels the effects of the good, or ill humour of the master in common with the
rest; when the school-hour is over, they
are all let loose to play together; he will
in general like the same games that others
do, and be most delighted when they are
noisiest, when they happen to be in the
best humour, in the hottest part of the

game, on the finest days, or in the pleasant-
est places: they will have the same joyous
breakings-up for the holidays, and will often on some bright morning stroll out in
search of unknown good, and return home
tired and disappointed together. Would
it not be strange if this constant fellow-
ship of joys and sorrows did not produce in him some sensibility to the good
or ill fortune of his companions,
and some real good-will towards them?
The greatest part of our pleasures depend
upon habit: and as those which arise from
acts of kindness and disinterested attachment to others are the most common, the
most lasting, the least mixed with evil of
all others, as a man devoid of all attachment to others, whose heart was thoroughly hard and insensible to every thing but
his own interest would scarcely be able to
support his existence, (for in him the spring
and active principle of life would be gone)
it follows that we ought to cultivate sentiments of generosity and kindness for others

out of mere selfishness. The obligations
to the practice of virtue really depend on
it's contributing to the original object of
our nature, our own proper happiness:
for no man is bound to sacrifice his own
ultimate welfare to any foreign consideration whatever. The advantages of virtue
are however to be derived, like those of any
liberal art, from the immediate gratification attending it, from it's necessary effect
on the mind, and not from a gross calcu-
lation of self-interest. This effect must
be the greatest, where there is the most
love of virtue for it's own sake, as we
become truly disinterested, and generous.
Therefore as the habit of generous concern
for others, and readiness to promote their
welfare cannot be broken in upon at will
in every particular instance where our immediate interest might require it, it becomes
necessary to disregard all such particular,
accidental advantages for the sake of the
general obligation, and thus confirm habit
into principle.

Whatever may be the manner in which we first acquire disinterested feelings, I do not think that much good can be done by tracing these feelings back again to a selfish origin, and leaving virtue no other basis to rest upon than a principle of refined self-interest, by setting on foot a sort of game at hide-and-seek between the *reasons* and *motives* to virtue. Without stopping to inquire whether the effect of this theory upon the mind would be to produce much true generosity, or disinterested simplicity of character, there can be no doubt but that this end must be attained much more effectually as far as the philosophical theory, or a belief of certain abstract distinctions will ever influence our habitual principles of action *, by shewing to man that his na-

---

* The question whether abstract or merely intellectual ideas have ever much influence on the conduct has not been fairly stated. The point is not whether an abstract proposition (no matter whether true or false) of which I became convinced yesterday, will be able to overturn all my previ-

c

ture is originally and essentially disinterested,
that as a voluntary agent, he must be a dis-

ous habits, and prejudices, but whether ideas of
this kind may not be made the foundation of inveterate prejudices themselves and the strongest principles of action. The ideas concerning religion are
of a sufficiently abstract nature : and yet it will not
be disputed that early impressions of this kind have
some influence on a man's future conduct in life.
Two persons accidentally meeting together, and
who had never seen one another before shall conceive
a more violent antipathy to each other in consequence of a dispute on religion or politics than they
might have done from having been personally at
variance half their lives. It is objected that this
proceeds from wounded vanity. But why is our
vanity more easily irritated upon these subjects than
upon any other but from the importance attached to
them by the understanding ? Questions of morality
do not always excite the same violent animosity ; and
this I think is because they do not so properly admit
of dispute in themselves, also because they are not so
often made the instruments of cabal, and power,
and therefore depend less on opinion, or the number
of votes, and because every one appealing to his
own breast for the truth of his opinion attributes
the continuance of the contest not to any want of

interested one; that he could neither desire,
nor will, nor pursue his own happiness but
for the possession of faculties which neces-

force in his own arguments, but to a want of proper feelings in his opponent.—I will add here a re-
mark in some measure connected with the last mentioned observation, that the reason why men are generally more anxious about the opinion entertained
of their understanding than their honesty is not so
much that they really think this last of less consequence as that a man always believes himself to
be the best judge of what passes in his own breast.
He therefore thinks very little the better of himself
for the good opinion of others. Indeed he considers
their suffrages in this respect as a sort of imper-
tinence at best, as implying some doubt upon the
subject: and as to their direct censures, he will always find some feelings, or motives in his own
mind, or some circumstances with which they
are not acquainted, which will in his opinion make
a total difference in the case. With respect to man-
ners, and those moral qualities which are deno-
minated *pleasing*, these again depend on the judgment of others; and we find the same jealousy of
the opinions of others manifested with respect to
these as with respect to our sense, wit, &c.

sarily give him an interest out of himself in the happiness of others; that personal identity neither does, nor can imply any positive communication between a man's future, and present self, that it does not give him a mechanical interest in his future being, that man when he *acts* is always absolutely independent of, uninfluenced by the feelings of the being *for whom he acts*, whether this be himself, or another; lastly, that all morality, all rational, and voluntary action, every thing undertaken with a distinct reference to ourselves or others must relate to the future, that is, must have those things for it's object which can only act upon the mind by means of the imagination, and must naturally affect it in the same manner, whether they are thought of in connection with our own future being, or that of others.

I have thought upon this subject so long, and it has sunk into my mind I may say so deeply in the single abstract form which appears to me to explain almost every other view which can be taken of it, that I cannot without difficulty bring myself to consider it separately or in detail; and I am sure that many things will appear to others very imperfectly and obscurely expressed which appear to me evident truisms from having been accustomed to refer a number of particular observations, and subordinate trains of feeling, which I have forgotten, to that general form of reasoning. However I hope that the simplicity of the principle itself which must be either logically and absolutely true, or not at all will make it sufficiently intelligible if it be stated with tolerable accuracy.

All voluntary action, that is all action proceeding from a will, or effort of the mind to produce a certain event must relate to the future, or to those things, the existence of which is problematical, undetermined, and therefore capable of being affected by the means made use of with a view to their production, or the contrary. But that which is future, which does not yet exist can excite no interest in itself, nor act upon the mind in any way but by means of the imagination. The direct primary motive, or impulse which determines the mind to the volition of any thing must therefore in all cases depend on the *idea* of that thing as conceived of by the imagination, and on the idea solely. For the thing itself is a non-entity. By the very act of it's being *willed*, it is supposed not to exist. It neither is any thing, nor can be the cause of any thing. We are never interested in the things themselves which are the real, ultimate, practical objects of volition : the feelings of desire, aversion, &c. connected with voluntary action are always excited by the ideas of those things before they exist. The true impulse to voluntary action can only exist in the mind of a being capable of foreseeing the consequences of things, of being

interested in them from the imaginary impression thus made upon his mind, and of
making choice of the means necessary to produce, or prevent what he desires or dreads.
This distinction must be absolute and uni-
versally applicable, if it is so at all. The
motives by which I am impelled to the pursuit of my own welfare can no more be the
result of a direct impression of the thing
which is the object of desire, or aversion, of
any positive communication between my
present, and future feelings, or of a sort of
hypostatical union between the interest of
the being acting, and the being acted upon,
than the motives by which I am interested
in the welfare of others can be so. It is true
I have a real, positive interest in my actual
feelings which I have not in those of others.
But actual pleasure, and pain are not the
objects of voluntary action. It can be to
no purpose, it is downright nonsense to
will that which actually exists, which is
impressed on my senses to exist, or not to
exist, since it will exist neither more nor

less for my willing it, or not willing it.
Our shrinking from that which gives us pain
could not in any respect be considered as an
act of volition, or reason, if we did not
know that the same object which gives us
pain will continue to give us pain while
we remain in contact with it. The mere
mechanical movement which generally accompanies much pain does not appear to
me to have any thing more to do with self-
love properly so called than the convulsive
motions or distortions of the muscles caused by bodily disease.——In other words the
object of volition is never the cause of volition. The motive, or internal impression impelling me to the pursuit of any
object is by the supposition incompatible
with any such interest as belongs to the actual enjoyment of any good, or to the idea
of *possession*. The real object of any particular volition is always a mere physical
consequence of that volition, since it is
willed for that very reason that otherwise
it would not exist at all, and since the ef-

fect which the mind desires to produce by any voluntary action must be subsequent to that action. It cannot therefore exert any power over my present volitions, and actions, unless we suppose it to act before it exists, which is absurd. For there is no faculty in the mind by which future impressions can excite in it a presentiment of themselves in the same way that past impressions act upon it by means of memory. When we say that future objects act upon the mind by means of the imagination, it is not meant that such objects exercise a real power over the imagination, but merely that it is by means of this faculty that we can foresee the probable or necessary consequences of things, and are interested in them.

I hardly know how to insist on a point so plain in itself that it cannot be made plainer by any kind of reasoning. I only wish to define the sense of the general position as strictly as I can, and to guard if possible against any mistake arising from ambiguity of expression. For nothing but the certainty of absolute proof, and of having avoided every error of this sort can overcome the reluctance of the mind to admit fully and in all it's consequences a distinction, which however simple in the abstract goes to the direct subversion of one of the most deeply rooted feelings of the human mind, namely that of the essential difference between the interest we have in promoting our own welfare by all the means in our power, and that which we take in promoting the welfare of others. Almost every one has a feeling that he has a real interest in the one, but that his interest in the other is merely imaginary; that his interest in the one is absolute and independent of himself, that it exists with the same force whether he feels it, or not, whether he pursues, or neglects it, that it is a part of himself, a bond from which he cannot free himself without changing his being, whereas the interest which he takes in the welfare of others is a voluntary interest, taken up and dismissed at pleasure, and which exists no longer than he feels it; that his interest in his own welfare, however distant, must affect *him* equally at present, since he is really the same being who is to enjoy, or suffer hereafter, but that with respect to the feelings of pleasure, or pain which another is to enjoy or suffer, he neither has any direct present interest, nor can have an indirect future interest in them: they are nothing to him. This is the common feeling; and it is perhaps not less common to the most generous than to the most narrow and selfish minds: for a man of a generous disposition will take pleasure in sacrificing his own immediate interest considering it as a real sacrifice, and will be fond of exulting in his superiority to the gross influence of selfish motives. If however the distinction above insisted on with respect to voluntary action be any thing more than a play of words without meaning, the whole of this feeling must be utterly false, and ground-

less. For the mind can take, it can have
no interest in any thing, that is an object
of practical pursuit, but what is strictly
imaginary : it is absurd to suppose that it
can have a *real* interest in any such object
directly whether relating to ourselves, or
others (this has been I trust sufficiently
shewn already) : neither can the reality of
my future interest in any object give me a
real interest in that object at present, unless
it could be shewn that in consequence of
my being the same individual I have a necessary sympathy with my future sensations
of pleasure or pain, by which means they
produce in me the same mechanical impulses as if their objects were really present.
The puncture of a pin causing an irritation
in the extremity of one of the nerves is sensibly felt along the whole extent of that
nerve ; a violent pain in any of the limbs
disorders the whole frame ; I feel at the
same moment the impressions made on opposite parts of my body ; the same conscious principle pervades every part of me, it

is in my hands, my feet, my eyes, my ears
at the same time, or at any rate is immediately affected by whatever is impressed on
all these, it is not confined to this, or that
organ for a certain time, it has an equal
interest in the whole sentient system, nothing that passes in any part of it can be
indifferent to me. Here we have a distinct idea of a real individuality of person, and a consequent identity of interests.
Till some such diffusive conscious principle can be shewn to exist, producing a real
connection between my future sensations
and present impulses, collecting, and unit-
ing the different successive moments of my
being in one general representative feeling of self-interest as the impressions made
on different parts of my body are all conveyed to one common principle of thought,
it is in vain to tell me that I have the same
interest in my future sensations as if they
were present, because I am the same individual. However nearly allied, however
similar I may be to my future self, what-

ever other relation I may bear to that self, so
long as there is not this intercommunity of
thoughts and feelings, so long as there is an
absolute separation, an insurmountable
barrier fixed between the present, and the
future, so that I neither am, nor can possibly be affected at present by what I am
to feel hereafter, I am not to any moral or
practical purpose the *same* being. Natural
impossibilities cannot be made to give way
to a mere courtesy of expression. "But
I know that I shall become that being."
Then my interest in it is founded on that
knowledge, and not on an event which not
only is not felt by my mind, but is itself
yet to come, viz. the transition of my present into my future being. How does it
signify to me what I shall hereafter feel, or
how can it influence my present conduct, or
how ought it to do so but because, and in
as far as, I have some idea of it beforehand*?

* The distinction between the motives to action
and the *reasons* for it cannot affect the argument here
insisted on. When it is said, that though I am not

The injury that I may do to my future
interest will not certainly by any kind of
reaction return to punish me for my neg-
lect of my own happiness.   In this sense,
I am always free from the consequences
of my actions.——The interests of the being
who acts, and of the being who suffers are
never one.   They are not swayed by the
influence of the same causes either directly,
or by mechanical sympathy.   The good
which is the object of pursuit can never
coexist with the motives which make it an
object of pursuit.   The good which any
being pursues is always at a distance from
him.   His wishes, his exertions are always excited by " an airy, notional good,"
by the idea of good, not the reality.   But

really governed by such and such motives, I ought
to be governed by them, this must mean (or it
means nothing) that such would be the effect of a
proper exertion of my faculties.   The obligation to
act in this or that manner must therefore be deduced
from the nature of those faculties, and the *possibility*
of their being impressed in a certain manner by certain objects.

for this there could be no desire, no pursuit of any thing. We cannot strive to
obtain what we already possess: we cannot
give to that which already exists a double
reality. My real interest is not therefore
something which I can handle, which is
to be felt, or seen, it is not lodged in the
organs of hearing, or taste, or smell, it is
not the subject of any of the senses, it is
not in any respect what is commonly understood by a real, substantial interest.
On the contrary, it is fundamentally, and
in it's origin and by it's very nature the creature of reflection, and imagination ; and
whatever can be made the subject of these,
whether relating to ourselves or others, may
also be the object of an interest powerful
enough to become the motive of volition
and action. If it should be asked then
what difference it can make to me whether
I pursue my own welfare, or entirely neg-
lect it, what reason I can have to be at all
interested in it, I answer that according to
the selfish hypothesis I do not see any.

But if we admit that there is something in the very idea of good, or evil, which naturally excites desire or aversion, which is in itself the proper motive of action, which impels the mind to pursue the one and to avoid the other by a true moral necessity, then it cannot be indifferent to me whether I believe that any being will be made happy or miserable in consequence of my actions, whether this be myself or another. I naturally desire and pursue my own good (in whatever this consists) simply from my having an idea of it sufficiently warm and vivid to excite in me an emotion of interest, or passion; and I love and pursue the good of others, of a relative, of a friend, of a family, a community, or of mankind for just the same reason.

The scheme of which I have here endeavoured to trace the general outline differs from the common method of accounting for the origin of our affections in this, that it supposes what is personal or selfish in our

D

affections to be the growth of time and habit, and the principle of a disinterested love of good as such, or for it's own sake without any regard to personal distinctions to be the foundation of all the rest. In this sense self-love is in it's origin a perfectly disinterested, or if I may so say *impersonal* feeling. The reason why a child first distinctly wills or pursues his own good is not because it is *his*, but because it is *good*. For the same reason he prefers his own gratification to that of others not because he likes himself better than others, but because he has a more distinct idea of his own wants and pleasures than of theirs. Independently of habit and association, the strength of the affection excited is in proportion to the strength of the idea, and does not at all depend on the person to whom it relates except indirectly and by implication. A child is insensible to the good of others not from any want of good-will towards them, or an exclusive attachment to self, but for want of knowing better. Indeed he can neither be attached to his own interest nor that of others but in consequence of knowing in what it consists. It is not on that account the less natural for him to seek to obtain personal pleasure, or to avoid personal pain after he has felt what these are. We are not born benevolent, that is we are not born with a desire of we know not what, and good wishes for we know not whom: neither in this sense are we born with a principle of self-love, for the idea of self is also acquired. When I say therefore that the human mind is naturally benevolent, this does not refer to any innate abstract idea of good in general, or to an instinctive desire of general indefinite unknown good but to the natural connection between the idea of happiness and the desire of it, independently of any particular attachment to the person who is to feel it.

There is a great difference between the general love of good which implies a knowledge of it, and a general disposition to the

love of good, which does not imply any
such thing. It is necessary to keep this
distinction in our minds, or the greatest
confusion will ensue. It is the general
property of iron to be attracted by the
loadstone, though this effect can only take
place in consequence of the loadstone's
being brought near enough to it, nor is any
thing more meant by the assertion. The
actual desire of good is not inherent in the
mind of man, because it requires to be
brought out by certain accessory objects
or ideas, but the disposition itself, or property of the mind which makes him liable
to be so affected by certain objects is inherent
in him and a part of his nature, as sensibility to pleasure and pain will not be de-
nied to be natural to man, though the actual feelings of pleasure and pain can only
be excited in him by the impression of certain external objects. The love of my
own particular good must precede that of
the particular good of others, because I
am acquainted with it first: the love of

particular must precede that of general
good whether my own, or another's, or the
general good of mankind for the same reason. I do not therefore originally love
my own particular positive good as a por-
tion of general good, or with a distinct reference in my mind to the good of the
whole; for I have as yet no idea of nor
any concern about the whole. But I love
my own particular good as consisting in
the first conception I have of some one
desirable object for the same reason, for
which I afterwards love any other known
good whether my own, or another's, whether conceived of as consisting in one or
more things, that is because it possesses
that essential property common to all good,
without which it would cease to be good
at all, and which has a general tendency
to excite certain given affections in my
mind. I conceive that the knowledge of
many different sorts of good must lead to
the love or desire of all these, and that this
knowledge of various good must be accom-

panied with an intermediate, composite, or indefinite idea of good, itself the object of desire, because retaining the same general nature: now this is an abstract idea. This idea will no doubt admit of endless degrees of indefiniteness according to the number of things, from which it is taken, or to which it is applied, and will be refined at last into a mere word, or logical definition. In this case it will owe all it's power as a motive to action to habit, or association; for it is so immediately or in itself no longer than while it implies a sentiment, or real feeling representative of good, and only in proportion to the degree of force and depth which this feeling has.*

---

* Similarity has been defined to be *partial* sameness. Curve lines have a general resemblance, or analogy to one another as such. Does this resemblance then consist in their being partially the same ? This may be said where the difference arises from drawing out the same sort of curve to a greater extent because by adding to the shorter curve I can make it equal to the other. But I cannot by adding any other line to an oval convert it into a circle, be-

The same objection evidently applies to
the supposition either of an original prin-

cause these two sorts of curves can never coincide
even in their smallest conceivable parts. It should
seem then that their similarity is not to be deduced
from partial sameness, or their having some one
thing exactly the same, common to them both. But
they have the same general nature as curves. True:
but in what does this abstract identity consist? Is it
not the same with similarity? So that we return to
the same point from which we set out. I confess no
light appears to me to be thrown on the subject by
saying that it is partial identity. The same sort of
reasoning is applicable to the question whether all
good is not to be resolved into one simple principle,
or essence, or whether all that is really good or pleasurable in any sensation is not the same identical
feeling, an infusion of the same leven of good, and
that all the rest is perfectly foreign to the nature of
good and is merely the form or vehicle in which it is
conveyed to the mind. I cannot however persuade
myself that our sensations differ only as to more, or
less; or that the pleasure derived from seeing a fine
picture, or hearing a fine piece of music, that the
gratification derived from doing a good action and
that which accompanies the swallowing of an oyster
are in reality and at bottom the same pleasure. The
liquor tastes of the vessel through which it passes.

ciple of general comprehensive benevolence,
or of general and comprehensive self-love.
They both suppose the mind to have attained an indefinite power of abstraction

It seems most reasonable to suppose that our feelings
differ in their nature according to the nature of the
objects by which they are excited, though not necessarily in the same proportion, as objects may excite
very distinct ideas which have little or nothing to do
with feeling. Why should there be only *two* sorts of
feeling, pleasure and pain? I am convinced that any
one who has reflected much on his own feelings must
have found it impossible to refer them all to the same
fixed invariable standard of good or evil, or by throw-
ing away the mere husk and refuse without losing any
thing essential to the feeling to arrive at some one sim ·
ple principle, the same in all cases, and which determines by it's quantity alone the precise degree of
good or evil in any sensation. Some sensations are
*like* others; this is all we know of the matter, and all
that is necessary to form a class, or *genus*. The contrary method of reasoning appears to proceed on a
supposition that things differing at all in kind must
differ *in toto*, must be quite different from each other;
so that a resemblance in kind must imply an absolute
coincidence in part, or in as far as the things resemble one another.---See USHER on the Human Mind,

which is not it's natural state. Both the
one and the other must be made up of
many actual pleasures and pains, of many
forgotten feelings and half-recollections,
of hopes and fears and insensible desires:
the one, that is, a sentiment of general
benevolence can only arise from an habitual cultivation of the natural disposition
of the mind to sympathize with the feelings
of others by constantly taking an interest in
those which we know, and imagining others
that we do not know, as the other feeling of
abstract self-interest, that is in the degree
in which it generally subsists, must be
caused by a long narrowing of the mind
to our own particular feelings and interests, and a voluntary insensibility to
every thing which does not immediately
concern ourselves. It is this excessive attachment to our own good because it is
ours, or for the sake of the abstract idea,
which has no immediate connection with
a real imagination of our own pleasures
and pains, that I consider as a purely arti-

ficial feeling and as proper selfishness; not
that love of self which first or last is derived from a more immediate knowledge of
our own good and is a natural consequence
of the general love of good as such. So
of our attachment to others; for the general principle as exerted with respect to
others admits of the same modifications
from habit as when it has a merely selfish
direction. Our affections settle upon
others as they do upon ourselves: they
pass from the thing to the person. " I
hate to fill a book with things that all the
world knows;" or I might here give a very
elaborate and exact account taken from
twenty different authors of the manner in
which this transition takes place. I do not
see how ideas are the better for being often
repeated. Suffice it to say that in all these
cases of habitual attachment the motives
to action do not depend so much on a real
interest in the thing which is the object of
pursuit as on a general disposition to serve
that particular person occasioned by a pre-

vious habit of kind offices and by transferring the feeling of a real interest in a number of things conducive to that person's welfare to the abstract idea of his good in general.
I leave it with the reader to apply this to
the cases of friendship, family attachments,
the effects of neighbourhood &c. and to
consider the feuds, the partialities, the an-
tipathies produced by these attachments,
and the consequent unwillingness to attend
to the natural feelings of compassion, humanity, and the love of justice : and then
let him see if the same process, that is the
ingrafting a general, or abstract interest on
an habitual positive feeling will not account in the same way for the effects of
self-love, without supposing this last as an
exclusive principle to be natural to the
human mind. For my own part, I believe that the cases are exactly parallel.
Thus we may consider self-love as bearing
the same relation to family affection as this
does to the more general love of our neighbour, as the love of onr neighbour does to

that of our country, or as the love of our country does to that of mankind. The love of mankind is here to be taken for an already given, definite, and to a certain degree *associated* feeling. The comparison might be instituted with a slight shade of difference between self-love, the love of a relative or friend, of a neighbour, and of an entire stranger. It is in proportioning our anxiety to promote the welfare of any of these to our sense of the use our assistance may be of, to use a well known phrase, *without respect of persons,* that what may be called the *natural* balance of our affections seems to consist. By the bye, this supposes that our insensibility to the feelings of others does not arise from an unwillingness to sympathise with them, or a habit of being stupidly engrossed by our own interests. Whether there may not be some higher principle of our general nature in conformity to which our sentiments and actions with respect to others should be voluntarily regulated, according to the same rule by which gross animal appetite is subjected to rational self-interest, may be made the subject of a future inquiry. All that is necessary to my present purpose is to have made it appear that the principles of natural self-love and natural benevolence, of refined self-love and refined benevolence are the same; that if we admit the one, we must admit the other; and that whatever other principles may be combined with them, they must stand, or fall together.

It is not therefore my intention to puzzle myself or my readers with the intricacies of a debtor and creditor account between nature and habit. Whatever the force of habit may be, however subtle and universal it's influence, it is not every thing, not even the principal thing. Before we plant, it is proper to know the nature of the soil, first that we may know whether it is good for any thing, secondly that we may know what it is good for. On these two questions will depend the

sort of cultivation we bestow upon it. After this is settled, it is idle to dispute how
much of the produce is owing to cultivation, and how much to the nature of the soil.
We should only be sure of having made the
best use of it we can. But we cannot be
sure of this till we know what it is naturally capable of  I will however lay down
two general maxims on this subject which
will not admit of much controversy. First,
when there is no natural connection between any two things which yet have been
supposed inseparable from a confused association of ideas, it is possible to destroy
this illusion of the imagination by rational
distinction, and consequently to weaken
the force of the habitual feeling which is
confirmed and rendered permanent by the
conviction of the understanding. Thus,
a principle of general self-interest has been
supposed inseparable from individuality,
because a feeling of immediate consciousness does essentially belong to certain individual impressions, and this feeling of

consciousness, of intimate sympathy, or of absolute self-interest has been transferred by custom and fancy together to the abstract idea of self. It is therefore of some use to separate these ideas, or to shew that there is no foundation in reason or the nature of things for a very strong prejudice which has been conceived to arise immediately out of them. The mind must be drawn together, must be contracted and shrunk up within itself by the mere supposition of this perpetual unity with itself and intense concentration of self-interest. Secondly, where this natural connection is wanting, that is, where the habitual connection of certain feelings with certain ideas does not arise from a predisposition in the mind to be affected by certain objects more than others, but from the partilar direction which has been given to the mind or a more frequent association between those feelings and ideas, a contrary habit may be produced by giving the mind a different direction, and bestowing a greater share of attention on other objects. It cannot be a matter of indifference then whether the faculty by which I am originally interested in the welfare of others is the same as that by which I am interested in my own welfare, or whether I am naturally incapable of feeling the least interest in the welfare of others except from it's indirect connection with my own. Habit is by it's nature to a certain degree arbitrary, and variable, the original disposition of the mind, it's tendency to acquire or persevere in this or that habit is alone fixed and invariable*. As however the force of previous habit is and always must be on the side

* It is a gross mistake to consider all habit as necessarily depending on association of ideas. We might as well consider the strength which is given to a muscle by habitual exertion as a case of the association of ideas. The strength, delicacy, &c. given to any feeling by frequent exercise is owing to habit. When any two feelings, or ideas are often repeated in connection, and the properties belonging to the one are by this means habitually transferred to the other, this is association.

of selfish feelings, it is some consolation to
think that the force of the habit we may
oppose to this is seconded by reason, and
the natural disposition of the mind, and that
we are not obliged at last to establish generosity and virtue, "lean pensioners" on
self-interest.*

* " Ainsi se forment les premiers liens qui l'unis-
sent" [le jeune homme] " à son espèce. En diri-
geant sur elle sa sensibilité naissante ne craignez pas
qu'elle embrassera d'abord tous les hommes, & que
ce mot de *genre-humain* signifiera pour lui quelque
chose. Non, cette sensibilité se bornera première-
ment à ses semblables, & ses semblables ne seront
point pour lui des inconnus, mais ceux avec lesquels
il a des liaisons, ceux que l'habitude lui a rendus
chers, ou nécessaires, ceux qu'il voit évidemment
avoir avec lui des manières de penser & de sentir
communes, ceux qu'il voit exposés aux peines qu'il
a souffertes, & sensibles aux plaisirs qu'il a goutés ;
ceux, en un mot, en qui l'identité de nature plus
manifestée lui donne une plus grande disposition à
aimer. Ce ne sera qu'après avoir cultivé son naturel
en milles maniéres, après bien des réflections sur ses
propres sentimens, & sur ceux qu'il observera dans

E

I have thus far attempted to shew by a logical deduction that the human mind is naturally disinterested: I shall at present try to shew the same thing somewhat differently, and more in detail.

To suppose that the mind is originally determined in it's choice of good and rejection of evil solely by a regard to self is to suppose a state of *indifference* to both, which would make the existence of such a feeling as self-interest utterly impossible. If there were not something in the very notion of good, or evil which naturally made the one an object of immediate desire and the other of aversion, it is not

les autres, qu'il pourra parvenir à généraliser ses notions individuelles sous l'idée abstraite d'humanité & joindre à ses affections particuliéres celles qui peuvent l'identifier avec son espèce." Emile, t. 2, p. 192.—It is needless to add any thing on this passage. It speaks for itself.

" L'amour du genre-humain n'est autre chose en nous que l'amour de la justice." Ibid. p. 248.

easy to conceive how the mind should
ever come to feel an interest in the prospect
of obtaining the one or avoiding the other.
It is great folly to think of deducing our
desire of happiness and fear of pain from a
principle of self-love, instead of deducing
self-love itself from our natural desire of
happiness and fear of pain. This sort of
attachment to self could signify nothing
more than a foolish complacency in our
own idea, an idle dotage, and idolatry of
our own abstract being; it must leave the
mind indifferent to every thing else, and
could not have any connection with the
motives to action, unless some one should
chuse to make it the foundation of a new
theory of the love of life and fear of death.
So long as the individual exists, and remains entire, this principle is satisfied. As
to the manner in which it exists, by what objects it shall be affected, whether it shall prefer one mode of being to another, all this is
left undetermined. If then by self-love be

meant a desire of one mode of being and aversion to another, or a desire of our own well-being, what is it that is to constitute this well-being? It is plain there must be something in the nature of the objects themselves which of itself determines the mind to consider them as desirable or the contrary previously to any reference of them to ourselves. They are not convert- ed into good and evil by being impressed on our minds, but they affect our minds in a certain manner because they are es- sentially good or evil. How shall we re- concile this with supposing that the nature of those objects or their effect on the mind is entirely changed by their being referred to this or that person? I repeat it that self-interest implies certain objects and feelings for the mind to be interested in: to suppose that it can exist separately from all such objects, or that our attach- ment to certain objects is solely deduced from, and regulated by our attachment to self is plain, palpable nonsense.

Take the example of a child that has been burnt by the fire, and consequently conceives a dread of it. This dread we will say does not consist simply in the apprehension of the pain itself abstractedly considered, but together with this apprehension of pain he connects the idea (though not a very distinct one) of himself as about to feel it. Let us consider in what way the intervention of this idea can be supposed to cause or increase his dread of the pain itself. In the first place then it is evident that the fire actually burns the child, not because he is thinking of himself, or of it's burning him, but because it is the nature of fire to burn and of the child's hand to feel pain, and his dislike of the pain while it actually exists is the immediate, necessary and physical consequence of the *sense* of pain, surely not an indirect and reflex result of the child's love to himself, or after-consideration that pain is an evil as it affects himself. Again I apprehend that after the actual pain has ceased, it continues to be thought of and is afterwards recollected as pain, or in other words, the feeling or sense of pain leaves a correspondent impression in the memory which adheres to the recollection of the object, and makes the child involuntarily shrink from it by the same sort of necessity, that is from the nature of the human mind and the recollected impression, and not from his referring it historically to his own past existence. In like manner I conceive that this idea of pain when combined by the imagination with other circumstances and transferred to the child's future being will still retain its original tendency to give pain, and that the recurrence of the same painful sensation is necessarily regarded with terror and aversion by the child, not from it's being conceived of in connection with his own idea, but because it is conceived of as pain\*. It

\* This account is loose enough. I shall endeavour to give a better, as to the manner in which ideas may be supposed to be connected with volition, should also be remembered as the constant principle of all our reasonings, that the impression which the child has of himself as the subject of future pain is never any thing more than an idea of imagination, and that he cannot possibly by any kind of anticipation feel that pain as a real sensation a single moment before it exists. How then are we to account for his supposed exclusive attachment to this ideal self so as to make that the real source of the dislike and dread which the apprehension of any particular pain to be inflicted on himself causes in the mind? There are two ways in which this may at first sight appear to be satisfactorily made out. The

---

at the end of this essay. In the mean time I wish the reader to be apprized, that I do not use the word *imagination* as contradistinguished from or opposed to reason, or the faculty by which we reflect upon and compare our ideas, but as opposed to sensation, or memory. It has been shewn above that by the word *idea* is not meant a merely abstract idea.

first is from the notion of personal identity:
this has been considered already and will
be again considered by and bye. The
other is something as follows. The child
having been burnt by the fire and only
knowing what the pain of a burn is from
his recollecting to have felt it himself, as
soon as he finds himself in danger of it again,
has a very vivid recollection of the pain it
formerly gave him excited in his mind;
and by a kind of sudden transposition
substituting this idea in the place of his
immediate apprehension, in thinking of
the danger to which he is exposed he confounds the pain he is to feel with that which
he has already actually felt, and in reality
shrinks from the latter. I mean that the
child strongly *recollects* that particular sort
of pain as it has affected himself, and as it is
not possible for him to have a recollection
of it's effect on any one else, he only re-
gards it as an evil in future in connection
with the same idea, or as affecting himself,
and is entirely indifferent to it as it is sup-

posed to affect any one else. Or in other words he remembers being burnt himself as an actual sensation, and he does not remember the actual sensations of any one but himself: therefore being able to trace back his present feelings to his past impressions, and struck with the extreme faintness of the one compared with the other, he gives way to his immediate apprehensions and imaginary fears only as he is conscious of, and dreads, the possibility of their returning into the same state of actual sensation again.

I do not deny that some such illusion of the imagination as I have here attempted to describe begins to take place very soon in the mind, and continues to acquire strength ever after from various causes. What I would contend for (and this is all that my argument requires) is that it is and can be nothing more than an illusion of the imagination, strengthening a difference in subordinate, indirect, collateral circumstances into an essential difference of kind.

The objection would indeed hold good if
it were true that the child's imaginary sympathy with the danger of another must be
derived as it were in a kind of direct line
from that other's actual sense of past pain,
or its immediate communication to his own
senses, which is absurd. It is not supposed
that the child can ever have felt the actual
pains of another as his own actual pains, or
that his sympathy with others is a real con-
tinuation and result of this original orga-
nic sympathy in the same way that his
dread of personal pain is to be deduced
from his previous consciousness of it. His
sympathy with others is necessarily the result of his own past experience: if he had
never felt any thing himself, he could not
posssibly feel for others. I do not know
that any light would be thrown upon the
argument by entering into a particular
analysis of the faculty of imagination; nor
shall I pretend to determine at what time
this faculty acquires sufficient strength to
enable the child to take a distinct interest

in the feelings of others. I shall content myself with observing that this faculty is necessary to the child's having any apprehension or concern about his own future interest, or that of others; that but for this faculty of multiplying, varying, extending, combining, and comparing his original passive impressions he must be utterly blind to the future and indifferent to it, insensible to every thing beyond the present moment, altogether incapable of hope, or fear, or exertion of any kind, unable to avoid or remove the most painful impressions, or to wish for or even think of their removal, to withdraw his hand out of the fire, or to move his lips to quench the most burning thirst; that without this faculty of conceiving of things which have not been impressed on his senses and of inferring like things from like, he must remain totally destitute of foresight, of self-motion, or a sense of self-interest, the passive instrument of undreaded pain and unsought-for pleasure, suffering and enjoying without resistance and without desire just as long as the different outward objects continued to act upon his senses, in a state of more than ideot imbecility; and that with this faculty enabling him to throw himself forward into the future, to anticipate unreal events and to be affected by his own imaginary interest, he must necessarily be capable in a greater or less degree of entering into the feelings and interests of others and of being consequently influenced by them. The child (by the time that his perceptions and actions begin to take any thing of a consistent form so that they can be made the subject of reasoning) being supposed to know from experience what the pain of a burn is, and seeing himself in danger a second time is immediately filled with terror, and strives either by suddenly drawing back his hand, catching hold of something, or by his cries for assistance to avoid the danger to which he is exposed. Here then his memory and senses present him with nothing more than certain external objects in

themselves indifferent, and the recollection
of extreme pain formerly connected with
the same or similar objects. If he had no
other faculties than these, he must stop here.
He would see and feel his own body moved
rapidly towards the fire, but his apprehensions would not outrun it's actual motion:
he would not think of his nearer approach
to the fire as a consequence of the force with
which he was carried along, nor dream of
falling into the fire till he found it actually
burning him. Even if it were possible for
him to foresee the consequence, it would
not be an object of dread to him; because
without a reasoning imagination he would
not and could not connect with the painted
flame before him the idea of violent pain
which the same kind of object had formerly
given him by it's actual contact. But in
fact he *imagines* his continued approach to
the fire till he falls into it; by his imagination he attributes to the fire a power to
burn, he conceives of an ideal self endued
with a power to feel, and by the force of

imagination solely anticipates a repetition
of the same sense of pain which he before
felt. If then he considers this pain which
is but an ideal sensation impressed on an
ideal being as an object of real, present,
necessary and irresistible interest to him,
and knowing that it cannot be avoided but
by an immediate exertion of voluntary
power, makes a sudden and eager effort to
avoid it by the first means he can think of,
why are we to suppose that the apprehension of the same pain to be inflicted on
another whom he must believe to be endued with the same feelings, and with
whose feelings he must be capable of sym-
pathizing in the same manner as with his
own imaginary feelings, should not affect
him with the same sort of interest, the
same sort of terrour, and impel him to the
same exertions for his relief? *

* I take it for granted that the only way to establish the selfish hypothesis is by shewing that our
own interest is in reality brought home to the mind
as a motive to action by some means or other by

Because, it is said, in his own case there is a natural deception, by which he confounds his future being with his past being and the idea of a future imaginary pain with the recollection of a past conscious pain. At any rate, this must be unconsciously: if the sense of present danger acts so powerfully on his mind as to bring back the recollection of a past sensation, and set that before him in the place of the real object of his fear, so that, while he is endeavouring to avoid an immediate danger, he is in fact thinking only of past suffering without his

which that of others cannot possibly affect it. This is unavoidable, unless we ascribe a particular genius of selfishness to each individual which never suffers his affections to wander from himself for a moment; or shall we suppose that a man's attachment to himself is because he has a long nose or a short one, because his hair is black or red, or from an unaccountable fancy for his own name, for all these make a part of the individual, and must be deemed very weighty reasons by those who think it self-evident that a man must love himself because he is himself?

perceiving this confusion of ideas, surely
the same thing must take place in a less degree with respect to others. If it be thought
necessary for him, before he can seek his
own future interest, to confound it with
his past interest by the violent transition
of an immediate apprehension into the
stronger recollection of an actual impression, then I say that by the same sort of sub-
stitution he will identify his own interest
with that of others, whenever a like obvious danger recals forcibly to his mind his
former situation and feelings, the lenses of
memory being applied in the one case to excite his sympathy and in the other to excite
personal fear, the objects of both being in
themselves equally imaginary and according to this hypothesis both perfectly indifferent. But I should contend that the assumption here made that the direct and
proper influence of the imagination is insufficient to account for the effects of personal fear, or of no force at all in itself
is without any foundation. For there is

no reason to be shewn why the ideas of
the imagination should not be efficient,
operative, as well as those of memory, of
which they are essentially compounded.
Their substance is the same. They are
of one flesh and blood. The same vital
spirit animates them both. To suppose
that the imagination does not exert a direct influence over human actions is to
reject the plain inference from the most
undoubted facts without any motive for
so doing from the nature and reason of
things. This notion could not have gained
ground as an article of philosophical faith
but from a perverse restriction of the use
of the word *idea* to abstract ideas, or external forms, as if the essential quality in
the feelings of pleasure, or pain must
entirely evaporate in passing through the
imagination; and again from associating
the word *imagination* with merely fictitious
situations and events, that is, such as never
will have a real existence, and as it is supposed never will, and which consequent-

ly do not admit of action. * Besides,
though it is certain that the imagination
is strengthened in it's operation by the
indirect assistance of our other faculties, yet as it is this faculty which must be
the immediate spring and guide of action,
unless we attribute to it an inherent, independent power over the will so as to make
it bend to every change of circumstances
or probability of advantage, and a power
at the same time of controuling the blind
impulses of associated mechanical feelings and of making them subservient to
the accomplishment of some particular
purpose, in other words without a power
of willing a given *end* for itself, and of em-
ploying the means immediately necessary to
the production of that end, because they
are perceived to be so, there could be neither volition, nor action, neither rational
fear nor steady pursuit of any object, neither
wisdom nor folly, generosity, or selfishness :
all would be left to the accidental concur-

* See the last note but one.

rence of some mechanical impulse with the immediate desire to obtain some very simple object, for in no other case can either accident or habit be supposed likely to carry any rational purpose into effect. To return however to what I have said above in answer to this objection, it is evident that all persons are more inclined to compassionate those pains and calamities in others by which they have been affected themselves, which proves that the operation of that principle, even supposing it to be the true one, is not confined to selfish objects. Our sympathy is always directly excited in proportion to our knowledge of the pain, and of the disposition and feelings of the sufferer. Thus with respect to ourselves we are little affected by the apprehension of physical pain which we have never felt and therefore can know little of; and we have still less sympathy with others in this case. Our incredulity and insensibility with respect to what others frequently suffer from the tooth-ache and other inci dental disorders must have been remarked by every one, and are even ludicrous from the excess to which they are carried. Give what account you will of it, the effect is the same;——our self-love and sympathy depend upon the same causes, and constantly bear a determinate proportion to each other, at least in the same individual. The same knowledge of any pain, which increases our dread of it, makes us more ready to feel for others who are exposed to it. When a boy I had my arm put out of joint, and I feel a kind of nervous twitching in it to this day whenever I see any one with his arm bound up in consequence of a similar accident. This part of my subject has been so well detailed by Smith and others that it is needless to insist on it farther. There are certain disorders which have a disgusting appearance, that shock and force attention by their novelty; but they do not properly excite our sympathy, or compassion, as they would do if we had ever been subject to them ourselves.

Children seem to sympathize more naturally with the outward signs of passion in
others without inquiring into the particular causes by which it is excited, whether it
is that their ideas of pain are more gross and
simple, therefore more uniform and more
easily substituted for each other, or that
grown-up persons, having a greater number of ideas and being oftener able to sympathize with others from knowing what they
feel, habitually make this knowledge the
foundation of their sympathy.*    In gene-

* The general clue to that ænigma, the character
of the French, seems to be that their feelings are
very imperfectly modified by the objects exciting
them.    That is, the difference between the several
degrees and kinds of feeling in them does not correspond as much as it does in most other people
with the different degrees and kinds of power in the
external objects.    They want neither feeling nor
ideas in the abstract; but there seems to be no
connection in their minds between the one and the
other.    Consequently their feelings want compass
and variety, and whatever else must depend on the
" building up of our feelings through the imagi-

ral it seems that those physical evils, which
we have actually experienced, and which

nation." The feelings of a Frenchman seem to be
all one feeling. The moment any thing produces a
change in him, he is thrown completely out of his
character, he is quite beside himself. This is perhaps in a great measure owing to their quickness of
perception. They do not give the object time to
be *thoroughly* impressed on their minds, their feelings are roused at the first notice of it's approach,
and if I may so express myself, fairly run away
from the object. Their feelings do not grapple
with the object. The least stimulus is sufficient to
excite them and more is superfluous, for they do
not wait for the impression, or stop to inquire what
degree or kind it is of There is not resistance
sufficient in the matter to receive those sharp inci-
sions, those deep, marked, and strongly rooted impressions, the traces of which remain for ever. From
whatever cause it proceeds, the sensitive principle
in them does not seem to be susceptible of the same
modification and variety of action as it does in
others; and certainly the outward forms of things
do not adhere to, do not wind themselves round
their feelings in the same manner. For any thing
that appears to the contrary, objects might be supposed to have no direct communication with the

from their nature must produce nearly the
same effect upon every one, must excite

internal sense of pleasure or pain, but to act upon
it through some intermediate, very confined organ,
capable of transmitting little more than the simple
impulse. But the same thing will follow, if we suppose the principle itself to be this very organ, that
is, to want comprehensiveness, elasticity, and plas-
tic force. (It is difficult to express this in English :
but there is a French word, *ressort*, which expresses
it exactly. This is possibly owing to their feeling
the want of it ; as there is no word in any other language to answer to the English word, *comfort*, I
suppose, because the English are the most uncom-
fortable of all people). It will rather follow from
what has been here said than be inconsistent with it
that the French must be more sensible of minute
impressions and slight shades of difference in their
feelings than others, because having, as is here
supposed, less real variety, a narrower range of feeling, they will attend more to the differences contained within that narrow circle, and so produce
an artificial variety. In short their feelings are
very easily set in motion and by slight causes, but
they do not go the whole length of the impression,
nor are they capable of combining a great variety of
complicated actions to correspond with the distinct

a more immediate and natural sympathy than those which depend on sentiment or

characters and complex forms of things. Hence they have no such thing as poetry. This however must not be misunderstood. I mean then that I never met with any thing in French that produces the same kind of feeling in the mind as the following passage. If there is any thing that belongs even to the same class with it, I am ready to give the point up.

 *Antony.*  *Eros*, thou yet behold'st me.

 *Eros.*  Ay, noble Lord.

 *Ant.*  Sometimes we see a cloud that's Drago-
  nish,

A vapour sometimes like a Bear, or Lion,

A tower'd Citadel, a pendant Rock,

A forked Mountain, or blue Promontory

With Trees upon't, that nod unto the World

And mock our Eyes with Air. Thou hast seen
  these Signs,

They are black Vesper's Pageants.

 *Eros.* Ay, my Lord.

 *Ant.* That which is now a Horse, even with a
  Thought

The rack dislimns, and makes it indistinct

As Water is in Water.

 *Eros.* It does, my Lord.

moral causes. It is however neither so
complete nor durable, as these last being

 *Ant.* My good Knave, *Eros,* now thy Cap-
  tain is
 Even such a body, &c.

It is remarkable that the French, who are a
lively people and fond of shew and striking images,
should be able to read and hear with such delight
their own dramatic pieces, which abound in nothing
but general maxims, and vague declamation, never
embodying any thing, and which would appear quite
tedious to an English audience, who are generally
considered as a dry, dull, plodding people, much
more likely to be satisfied with formal descriptions
and grave reflections. This appears to me to come
to the same thing that I have said before, namely,
that it is characteristic of the French that their
feelings let go their hold of things almost as soon as
the impression is made. Except sensible impressions therefore (which have on that account more
force, and carry them away without opposition
while they last) all their feelings are general; and
being general, not being marked by any strong distinctions, nor built on any deep foundation of inveterate associations, one thing serves to excite
them as well as another, the name of the general
class to which any feeling belongs, the words *plea-*

the creatures of imagination appeal more strongly to our sympathy, which is itself

*sure, charming, delicious,* &c. convey just the same meaning, and excite the same kind of emotion in the mind of a Frenchman, and at the same time do this more readily than the most forcible description of real feelings, and objects. The English on the contrary are not so easily moved with words, because being in the habit of retaining individual images and of brooding over the feelings connected with them, the mere names of general classes, or (which is the same thing) vague and unmeaning descriptions or sentiments must appear perfectly indifferent to them. Hence the French are delighted with Racine, the English (I mean some of them) admire Shakespear. Rousseau is the only French writer I am acquainted with (though he by the bye was not a Frenchman) who from the depth of his feelings, without many distinct images, produces the same kind of interest in the mind that is excited by the events and recollections of our own lives. If he had not true genius, he had at least something which was a very good substitute for it. The French generalise perpetually, but seldom comprehensively: they make an infinite number of observations, but have never discovered any great principle. They immediately perceive the analogy between a number

an act of the imagination, than mere physical evils can ever do, whether they relate
to ourselves or others. Our sympathy
with physical evil is also a more unplea-
sant feeling, and therefore submitted to
with more reluctance. So that it is necessary to take another circumstance into the
account in judging of the quantity of our

of facts of the same class, and make a general inference, which is done the more easily, the fewer
particulars you trouble yourself with ; it is in a good
measure the art of forgetting. The difficult part of
philosophy is, when a number of particular observations and contradictory facts have been stated,
to reconcile them together by finding out some
other distinct view of the subject, or collateral circumstance, applicable to all the different facts or
appearances, which is the true principle from which
when combined with particular circumstances they
are all derived. Opposite appearances are always
immediately incompatible with each other, and cannot therefore be deduced from the same immediate
cause, but must be accounted for from a combination of different causes, the discovery of which is an
affair of comprehension, and not of mere abstraction.

sympathy besides the two above mentioned, namely, the nature of the pain or it's fitness to excite our sympathy. This makes no difference in the question.

To say that the child recollects the pain of being burnt only in connection with his own idea, and can therefore conceive of it as an evil only with respect to himself, is in effect to deny the existence of any such power as the imagination. By the same power of mind which enables him to conceive of a past sensation as about to be re-excited in the same being, namely, himself, he must be capable of transferring the same idea of pain to a different person. He *creates* the object, he pushes his ideas beyond the bounds of his memory and senses in the first instance, and he does no more in the second. If his mind were merely passive in the operation, he would not be busy in anticipating a new impression, but would still be dreaming of the old one. It is of the very nature of the imagination to change the order in which things have been impressed on the senses, and to connect the same properties with different objects, and different properties with the same objects; to combine our original impressions in all possible forms, and to modify these impressions themselves to a very great degree. Man without this would not be a rational agent: he would be below the dullest and most stupid brute. It must therefore be proved in some other way that the human mind cannot conceive of or be interested in the pleasures or pains of others because it has never felt them.

The most subtle way of putting this objection is to represent the tendency of the child's apprehension of danger to deter him from going near the fire as caused not simply by the apprehension or idea itself, which they say would never have strength enough for a motive to action, but by his being able to refer that idea to an actual sensation in his own mind, and knowing that with respect to himself it will pass into the same state of serious reality again, if he ex-

poses himself to the same danger. Now
here we have nothing but a reflection on
a reflection. It is supposed that the direct
idea of a terrible and well-known pain has
no effect at all upon the mind, but that the
idea of this idea as about to be converted
into, or succeeded by the pain itself in the
same conscious being will immediately excite the strongest efforts to prevent it. Certainly the near expectation of the object of
your dread actually realized to the senses
strengthens the fear of it; but it strengthens
it through the imagination. Just as the
knowing that a person whom you wished
anxiously to see and had not seen for many
years was in the next room would make
you recall the impression of their face or
figure almost with the same vividness and
reality as if they were actually present.
The force then with which the mind anticipates future pain in connection with the
idea of continued consciousness can only
tend to produce voluntary action by making the idea stronger: but it could not have

this effect at all if it were not of the nature of all pain when foreseen by the mind
to produce a tendency that way, that is to
excite aversion, and a will to prevent it,
however slight this may sometimes be.
The sophism which lurks at the bottom of
this last objection seems to be the confounding the idea of future pain as the
cause or motive of action with the after-
reflection on that idea as a positive thing,
itself the object of action.   Finding in
many cases that the first apprehension and
momentary fear of danger was gone by, but
that the reason for avoiding it still remained
the same, the mind would be easily led to
seek for the true cause of action in something more fixed and permanent than the
fleeting ideas of remote objects, and to require that every object whether of desire or
aversion should have some stronger hold
on the individual than it's momentary effect on his imagination before it became an
object of serious pursuit, or the contrary.
But in rejecting the ideas of things as them-

selves the ultimate grounds and proper objects of action, and referring the mind to
the things themselves as the only solid basis of a rational and durable interest, what
do we do but go back to the first direct
idea of the object, which as it represents
that object is as distinct from any secondary reflection on, or oblique consciousness of, itself as an absolute thing, the object of thought, as a sensation can be different from an idea, or a present impression
from a future one. There is nothing in
the foregoing theory which has any tendency to overturn the fundamental distinctions between truth and falsehood, or the
common methods of judging what these are:
all the old boundaries and land-marks remain just where they were. It does not
surely by any means follow because the
reality of future objects can only be judged
of by the mind, that therefore it has no
power of distinguishing between the probable consequences of things, and what
can never happen, that it is to take every

impulse of will or fancy for truth, or because future objects cannot act upon the
mind from without, that therefore our ideas
cannot have any reference to, or properly
represent those objects, or any thing external to the mind, but must consist entirely
in the conscious contemplation of themselves.

There is another feeling in a great measure the same with the former, but distin-
guishable from it and still more strongly
connected with a sense of self-interest,
namely, that of continued personal identity. This has been already treated of:
I shall here resume the question once for
all, as it is on this that the chief stress of
the argument lies. The child seeing himself in danger of the fire does not think of
his present and future self as two distinct
beings, but as one and the same being: he
as it were *projects* himself forward into the
future, and identifies himself with his future being. He knows that he shall feel
his own future pleasures and pains, and

G

that he must therefore be as much interested in them as if they were present. In
thinking of the future, he does not conceive
of any change as really taking place in himself, or of any thing intermediate between
his present and future being, but considers
his future sensations as affecting that very
same conscious being in which he now
feels such an anxious and unavoidable interest. We say that the hand which the
child snatches back from the fire is the
same hand which but for his doing so
would the next moment be exposed to the
most excessive pain. But this is much more
true of that inward conscious principle which
alone connects the successive moments of
our being together, and of which all our
outward organs are but instruments, subject to perpetual changes both of action
and suffering. To make the difference of
time the foundation of an essential distinction and complete separation between his
present and future being as if this were
the only thing to be attended to is to op-

pose an unmeaning sophism to plain matter of fact, since mere distance of time does
*not* destroy individuality of consciousness.
He is the same conscious being now that
he will be the next moment, or the next
hour, or a month or a year hence. His
interests as an individual as well as his being must therefore be the same. At least
this must be the case as long as he retains
the consciousness of his past impressions
connecting them together in one uniform
or regular train of feeling: for the interruption of this sense of continued identity
by sleep, inattention or otherwise seems
from it's being afterwards renewed to prove
the point more clearly, as it seems to shew
that there is some deep inward principle
which remains the same in spite of all particular accidental changes.

The child does no doubt consider himself as the same being, or as directly and
absolutely interested in his own welfare,
as far as he can distinctly foresee the consequences of things to himself. But this

very circumstance of his identifying himself with his future being, of feeling for
this imaginary self as if it were incorpo-
rated with his actual substance, and weighed
upon the pulses of his blood is itself the
strongest instance that can be given of the
force of the imagination, which the advo-
cates of the selfish hypothesis would represent as a faculty entirely powerless.

No one, I should think, will be disposed seriously to maintain that this future
imaginary self is, by a kind of metaphysical transubstantiation, virtually embo-
died in his present being, so that his future impressions are indirectly communicated to him before-hand. For whatever
we may imagine, or believe concerning the
substance itself, or elementary principle in
which thought is supposed to reside, it is
plain that that principle as acted upon by
external objects, or modified by particular
actual thoughts and feelings (which alone
can be the motives of action, or can impel the mind in this, or that direction) is

perpetually changing; and it is also plain
that the changes which it has to undergo at
any time can have no possible effect on
those which it has previously undergone,
which may be the cause indeed but cannot
be the effect of subsequent changes. In
this sense the individual is never the same
for two moments together. What is true
of him at one time is never (that we know
of) exactly and particularly true of him at
any other time. It is idle to say that he
is the same being generally speaking, that
he has the same general interest. For he
is also a man in general; and this argument would prove that he has a general
interest in whatever concerns humanity.
Indeed the terms mean nothing as applied
to this question. The question is whether
the individual is the same being in such
sort or manner as that he has an equal, absolute interest in every thing relating to
himself, or that his future impressions affect
him as much and impel him to action with
the same mechanical force as if they were

actually present. This is so far from being true that his future impressions do not exert the smallest influence over his actions, they do not affect him mechanically in any degree. The catechism of this philosophy would run thus. You are necessarily interested in your future sensations? Yes. And why so? Because I am the same being. What do you mean by *the same being?* The same being is the same individual, that is, one who has the same interests, the same feelings, the same consciousness, so that whatever affects him at any one time must extend to his whole existence. He must therefore be at all times interested in it alike. Do you then feel your future sensations before they really exist? No. How then, if you do not feel them, can you be affected by them? Because as the same individual, &c. That is, by the very supposition the pain which the child is to suffer does not exist, of course he does not feel it, nor can he be moved, affected or interested by it as if it did: and yet in the same breath, by a shrewd turn of logic it is proved that as he is the same being, he must feel, be interested in and affected by it as much as he ever will. But then it will as shrewdly follow that withth is implication he is not the same being, for he cannot be affected in the same manner by an object before it is impressed on his senses that he is afterwards; and the fear or imaginary apprehension of pain is a different thing from the actual perception of it. There is just the same difference between feeling a pain yourself and believing that another will feel it.

I do request the reader to bear it in mind throughout the whole of this reasoning that when I say that the child *does not* feel, that he *is not* interested in his future sensations, and consider this as equivalent to his *having* no real or personal interest in them, I mean that he *never* feels or can be affected by them before-hand, that he is always necessarily cut off from every kind of communication with them, that they cannot possibly act upon his mind as motives to action; or excite in him any kind of impulse in any circumstances or any manner: and I conceive that it is no great stretch of speculative refinement to insist that without some such original faculty of being immediately affected by his future sensations more than by those of others, his relation to his future self, whatever that may be, cannot be made the foundation of his having a real positive interest in his future welfare which he has not in that of others. A general, or abstract, or reflex interest in any object implies either a previous positive interest in that object, or a natural capacity in the mind to be affected by it in the manner given. Thus I may be said to pursue any object from a general interest in it, though it excites no interest or emotion in my mind at the time, when I do this from habit, or when the impression has been so often repeated as to have produced a mechanical tendency to the pursuit of the object, which has no need of any new impulse to excite it. Or the same thing may be said with reference to my general nature as a voluntary agent. This implies that the object, in which I am supposed to be interested without being sensible of it, is in itself *interesting* to me, that it is an object in which I can and must necessarily be interested, the moment it is known to me; that I am interested generally in that whole class of objects, and may be said to be interested in this inclusively. To go farther than this, and say that the mind as the representative of truth is or ought to be interested in things as they are really and truly interesting in themselves, without any reference to the manner in which they immediately affect the individual, is to destroy at once the foundation of every principle of selfishness, which supposes that all objects are good or bad, desirable or the contrary solely from their connection with self. But I am tired of repeating the same thing so often; for " as to those that will not be at the pains of a little thought, no multiplication of words will ever suffice to make them understand the truth or rightly conceive my meaning."*

To return. Even if it were possible to establish some such preposterous connection between the same individual, as that, by virtue of this connection, his future sensations should be capable of transmitting their whole strength and efficacy to his present impulses, and of clothing ideal motives with a borrowed reality, yet such is the nature of all sensation, or absolute existence as to be incompatible with voluntary action. How should the reality of my future interest in any object be (by anticipation) the reason of my having a real interest in the pursuit of that object at present, when if it really existed I could no longer pursue it. The feelings of desire, aversion, &c. connected with voluntary action must

* Berkeley's Essay on Vision.

always be excited by the idea of the object
before it exists, and must be totally inconsistent with any such interest as belongs to
actual suffering or enjoyment.* The interest belonging to any sensation or real
object as such, or which arises as one may
say from the final absorption of the idea in
the object cannot have any relation to an
active or voluntary interest which necessarily implies the disjunction of these two
things: it cannot therefore be the original,
the parent-stock, the sole and absolute
foundation of an interest which is defined by it's connection with voluntary action.—Still it will be said that however difficult it may be to explain in what this
consists, there is a principle of some sort or
other which constantly connects us with
ourselves, and makes each individual the
same person distinct from every one else.
And certainly if I did not think it possible
to account satisfactorily for the origin of

* See page 22, and the following pages.

the idea of self, and the influence which
that idea has on our actions without loosen-
ing the foundation of the foregoing reasonings, I should give them up without a
question, as there is no reasoning which
can be safely opposed against a common
feeling of human nature left unexplained,
and without shewing in the clearest manner the grounds from which it may have
arisen. I shall proceed to state (as far as
is necessary to the present argument) in
what the true notion of personal identity
appears to me to consist; and this I believe
it will be easy to shew depends entirely
on the continued connection which subsists between a man's past and present feelings and not, *vice versâ*, on any previous
connection between his future and his present feelings, which is absurd and impossible.

Every human being is distinguished
from every other human being, both numerically, and characteristically. He
must be numerically distinct by the sup-

position: otherwise he would not be another individual, but the same. There is
however no contradiction in supposing
two individuals to possess the same absolute
properties: but then these original properties must be differently modified afterwards
from the necessary difference of their situations, or we must suppose them both to
occupy the same relative situation in two
distinct systems corresponding exactly
with each other. In fact every one is
found to differ essentially from every one
else, if not in original properties, in the
circumstances and events of their lives and
consequent ideas. In thinking of a number of individuals, I conceive of them all
as differing in various ways from one
another as well as from myself. They differ in size, in complexion, in features, in
the expression of their countenances, in
age, in the events and actions of their lives,
in situation, in knowledge, in temper, in
power. It is this perception or apprehension of their real differences that first

enables me to distinguish the several individuals of the species from each other,
and that seems to give rise to the most
general idea of individuality, as representing first positive number, and secondly the sum of the differences between
one being and another as they really
exist in a greater or less degree in nature,
or as they would appear to exist to an im-
partial spectator, or to a perfectly intelligent being. But *I* am not in reality more
different from others than any one individual is from any other individual ; neither
do I in fact suppose myself to differ really
from them otherwise than as they differ
from each other. What is it then that
makes the difference greater *to me*, or that
makes me feel a greater difference in passing from my own idea to that of any one
else than in passing from the idea of an
indifferent person to that of any one else?
Neither my existing as a separate being,
nor my differing from others is of itself
sufficient to constitute personality, or give

me the idea of self, since I might perceive others to exist, and compare their actual differences without ever having this idea.

Farther, individuality expresses not merely the absolute difference, or distinction between one individual and another, but also a relation, or comparison of that individual with itself, whereby we affirm that it is in some way or other the same with itself or one thing. In one sense it is true of all existences whatever that they are the same with themselves, that is they are what they are and not something else. Each thing is itself, it is that individual thing and no other, and each combination of things is that combination and no other. So also each individual is necessarily the same with himself, or in other words that combination of ideas which represents any individual person is that combination of ideas and not a different one. This is the only true and absolute identity which can be affirmed of any being; which it is plain does not arise from a comparison

of the different parts composing the general idea one with another, but each with
itself, or all of them taken together with
the whole. I cannot help thinking that
some idea of this kind is frequently at the
bottom of the perplexity which is felt by
most people who are not metaphysicians
(not to mention those who are) when they
are told that the man is not the same with
himself, their notion of identity being that
he is the same with himself in as far as he
is positively different from every one else.
They compare his present existence with
the present existence of others, and his
continued existence with the continued
existence of others. Thus when they say
that the man is the same being in general,
they do not mean that he is the same at
twenty that he is at sixty, but their general idea of him includes both these extremes, and therefore the same man, that
is collective idea, is both the one and the
other. This however is but a rude logic.
Not well understanding the process of dis-

tinguishing the same individual into different metaphysical sections to compare, col-
late, and set one against the other, (so awk-
wardly do we at first apply ourselves to the
analytic art!) to get rid of the difficulty,
the mind produces a *double* individual part
real and part imaginary, or repeats the same
idea twice over, in which case it is a contradiction to suppose that the one does not correspond exactly with the other in all it's parts.
There is no other absolute identity in the
case.

All individuals (or all that we name
such) are aggregates, and aggregates of
dissimilar things. Here then the question
is not how we distinguish one individual
from another, or a number of things from
a number of other things, which distinction
is a matter of absolute truth, but how we
come to confound a number of things together, and consider many things as the same,
which cannot be strictly true. This idea
must therefore relate to such a connection
between a number of things as determines
the mind to consider them as one whole,

each thing in that whole having a much nearer and more lasting connection with the rest than with any thing else not included in it, so that the degree of connection between the parts after all requires to be determined by annexing the name of the thing, that is collective idea, signified. (The same causes that determine the mind to consider a number of things as the same individual must of course imply a correspondent distinction between them and other things, not making part of that individual. The eye is not the same thing as the ear, it is a contradiction to call it so. Yet both are parts of the same body, which contains these and infinite other distinctions. The reason of this is that all the parts of the eye have evidently a distinct nature, a separate use, a greater mutual dependence on one another than on those of the ear, at the same time that the connection between the eye and ear as well as the rest of the body is still very great, compared to their connection with any other body of the same kind, which is none at all. Similarity is in general but a subordinate circumstance in determining this relation. For the eye is certainly more like the same organ in another individual than the different organs of sight and hearing are like one another in the same individual. Yet we do not, in making up the imaginary individual, associate our ideas according to this analogy, which of itself would answer no more purpose than the things themselves would, so separated and so reunited, but we think of them in that order in which they are mechanically connected together in nature, because it is on this order that depends their power of mutually acting and reacting on each other, of acting conjointly upon other things or of being acted upon by them. To give an instance which just occurs to me. Suppose there are two gold-headed canes standing together in the corner of the room. I of course consider each of them as the same cane. This is not from the similarity of the gold to the wood. But the two gold-heads together would not

if taken off at all answer the purpose of a cane, and the two canes together would be more than I should want. Nor is it simply from the contiguity of the parts, (for the canes themselves are supposed to touch one another) but from their being so united that by moving any part of one of them, I of necessity move the whole. The closest connection between my ideas is formed by that relation of things among themselves, which is most necessary to be attended to in making use of them, the common concurrence of many things to some given end: for example, my idea of the walking-stick is defined by the simplicity of the action necessary to wield it for that particular purpose. However, it seems hardly possible to define the different degrees or kinds of identity in the same thing by any general rule. Thus we say the same tree, the same forest, the same river, the same field, the same country, the same world, the same man, &c. The nature of the thing will best point out the

sense in which it is said to be the same.*

* The sum of the matter is this. Individuality may relate either to absolute unity, to the identity, or similarity of the parts of any thing, or to an extraordinary degree of connection between things neither the same nor similar. This laſt alone in fact determines the positive use of the word, at leaſt with respect to man, and other organized beings. (Indeed the term is hardly ever applied to other things in common language.) When I speak of the difference between one individual and another, this must refer ultimately to the want of such connection between them, or to my perceiving that a number of things are so connected as to have a mutual and intimate dependence on one another, making one individual, and that they are so *disconnected* with a number of other things as not to have the least habitual dependence upon or influence over them, which makes them two distinct individuals. As to the other distinctions between one individual and another, namely those of number and properties, the first of these subsists as necessarily between the parts of the individual, as between one individual and another, and the second frequently subsists in a much greater degree between those parts, than between different individuals. Two distinct individuals can certainly never be the

—I am not the same thing, but many different things. To insist on absolute simplicity
of nature as essential to individuality would
be to destroy all individuality : for it would

same : that is, supposing the number of parts in
each individual to be as 10, 10 can never make 20.
But neither can 10 ever be made into an unit ; so
that we should have ten individuals instead of one
by insisting on the absolute distinction of numbers.
When I say therefore that one individual differs from
another, I must be understood by implication to
mean, in some way in which the parts of that individual do *not* differ from each other or not by any means
in the same degree. The mind is however extreme-
ly apt to fasten on the distinctions of number and
properties where they co-exist with the other distinction, and almost loses sight of those distinctions
between things that have a very close connection
with each other. When therefore we include the
distinctions of number and properties in our account
of the difference between one individual and another, this can only be true in an absolute sense,
and not if it be meant to imply that the same distinctions do not exist in the same individual.—
This account is altogether very crude and unsatis-
factory.

lead to the supposition of as many distinct individuals, as there are thoughts, feelings, actions, and properties in the same being. Each thought would be a separate consciousness, each organ a different system. Each thought is a distinct thing in nature; and many of my thoughts must more nearly resemble the thoughts of others than they do my own sensations, for instance, which nevertheless are considered as a part of the same being. As to the continued identity of the whole being, that is the continued resemblance of my thoughts to my previous thoughts, of my sensations to my previous sensations and so on, this does not by any means define or circumscribe the individual, for we may say in the same manner that the species also is going on at the same time, and continues the same that it was. It is necessary to determine what constitutes the same individual at some given moment of time before we can say that he *continues* the same. Neither does the relation of cause and effect determine the point: the father of the child is not the child, nor the child the father. In this case there is an obvious reason to the contrary: but we make the same distinction where a proper succession takes place and the cause is entirely lost in the effect. We should hardly extend the idea of identity to the child before it has life, nor is the fly the same with the caterpillar. Here we again recur to likeness as essential to identity.

But to proceed to a more particular account of the origin of our idea of self, which is this relation of a thinking being to itself. This can only be known in the first instance by a consciousness of what passes in our own minds. I should say then that personality does not arise either from the being this, or that, from the identity of the thinking being with itself at different times or at the same time, or still less from being unlike others, which is not at all necessary to it, but from the peculiar

connection which subsists between the different faculties and perceptions of the same
conscious being, constituted as man is, so
that as the subject of his own reflection or
consciousness the same things impressed on
any of his faculties produce a quite different effect upon *him* from what they would
do if they were impressed in the same way
on any other being. Personality seems to be
nothing more than conscious individuality :
it is the power of perceiving that you are
and what you are from the immediate reflection of the mind on it's own operations, sensations, or ideas. It cannot be
affected in the same direct manner by the
impressions and ideas existing in the minds
of others: otherwise they would not be so
many distinct minds, but one and the same
mind; for in this sense the same mind will
be that in which different ideas and faculties have this immediate communication
with or power of acting and reacting upon
each other. If to this we add the relation
of such an inward conscious principle to a

certain material substance, with which it has the same peculiar connection and intimate sympathy, this combination will be the same person.

The visible impression of a man's own form does not convey to him the idea of personality any more than that of any one else; because as objects of sight they are both equally obvious and make the same direct impression on the eye; and the internal perception is in both cases equally incommunicable to any other being. It is the impinging of other objects against the different parts of our bodies, or of the body against itself so as to affect the sense of touch, that extends (though perhaps somewhat indirectly) the feeling of personal identity to our external form. The reason of which is that the whole class of tangible impressions, or the feelings of heat and cold, of hard and soft, &c. connected with the application of other material substances to our own bodies can only be produced by our immediate contact with them, that is, the body is necessarily the instrument by which these sensations are conveyed to the mind, for they cannot be conveyed to it by any impression made on the bodies of others; whereas, as an object of sight or where the body in general acts from without on that particular organ, the eye, the impression which it excites in the mind can affect it no otherwise than any similar impression produced by any other body must do. Afterwards no doubt the visible image comes in to confirm and give distinctness to the imperfect conclusions of the other sense*.

* I remember a story somewhere in the Arabian Nights of a man with a silver thigh. Why may not a fable serve for an illustration as well as any thing else? Metaphyfics themselves are but a dry romance. Now suppose this thigh to have been endued with a power of sensation and to have answered every other purpose of a real thigh. What difference would this make in it's outward appearance either to the man himself or to any one else? Or how by means of sight would he know it to be *his*

It is by comparing the knowledge that
I have of my own impressions, ideas, feelings, powers, &c. with my knowledge of
the same or similar impressions, ideas, &c.
in others, and with the still more imperfect conception that I form of what
passes in their minds when this is supposed
to be essentially different from what passes
in my own, that I acquire the general
notion of self. If I had no idea of what
passes in the minds of others, or if my ideas
of their feelings and perceptions were perfect representations, *i. e.* mere conscious
repetitions of them, all proper personal distinction would be lost either in pure self-
love, or in perfect universal sympathy.
In the one case it would be impossible for

thigh, more than it was? It would still look just
like what it did, a silver thigh and nothing more.
It's impression on the eye would not depend on it's
being a *sensible* substance, on it's having life in it,
or being connected with the same conscious principle as the eye, but on it's being a visible substance,
that is having extension, figure, and colour.

me to prefer myself to others as I should
be the sole object of my own consciousness; and in the other case I must love all
others as myself, because I should then be
nothing more than part of a whole, of
which all others would be equally mem-
bers with myself. I will here add once
more that this distinction subsists as necessarily and completely between myself and
those who most nearly resemble me as between myself and those whose character and
properties are the very opposite of mine: because it does not relate to the difference be
tween one being and another, or between one
object and another considered absolutely or
in themselves, but solely to the difference
of the manner and the different degrees of
force and certainty, with which, from the
imperfect and limited nature of our faculties, the same or different things affect us
as they act immediately upon ourselves, or
are supposed to act upon others. Indeed
the distinction becomes marked and intelligible in proportion as the objects or impres-

sions are intrinsically the same, as then it is impossible to mistake the true principle on which it is founded, namely the want of any direct communication between the feelings of one being and those of another. This will shew why the difference between ourselves and others must appear greater to us than that between other individuals, though it is not really so.

Considering mankind in this two-fold relation, as they are to themselves, or as they appear to one another, as the subjects of their own thoughts, or the thoughts of others, we shall find the origin of that wide and absolute distinction which the mind feels in comparing itself with others to be confined to two faculties, viz. *sensation*, or rather consciousness*, and *memory*. The operation of both these faculties is of

---

* To avoid an endless subtlety of distinction I have not here given any account of consciousness in general: but the same reasoning will apply to both.

a perfectly exclusive and individual nature; and so far as their operation extends (but no farther) is man a personal, or if you will, a selfish being. The sensation excited in me by a piece of red-hot iron striking against any part of my body is simple, absolute, terminating in itself, not representing any thing beyond itself, nor capable of being represented by any other sensation or communicated to any other being. The same sensation may indeed be excited in another by the same means, but this sensation does not imply any reference to, or consciousness of mine: there is no communication between my nerves, and another's brain, by means of which he can be affected with my sensations as I am myself. The only notice or perception which another can have of this sensation in me or which I can have of a similar sensation in another is by means of the imagination. I can form an imaginary idea of that pain as existing out of myself: but I can only feel it as a sensation when it is actually impressed on myself. Any impression made on another can neither be the cause nor object of sensation to me. The impression or idea left in my mind by this sensation, and afterwards excited either by seeing iron in the same state, or by any other means is properly an idea of memory. This idea necessarily refers to some previous impression in my own mind, and can only exist in consequence of that impression: it cannot be derived from any impression made on another. I do not *remember* the feelings of any one but myself. I may remember the objects which must have caused such or such feelings in others, or the outward signs of passion which accompanied them: these however are but the recollection of my own immediate impressions, of what I saw or heard; and I can only form an idea of the feelings themselves after they have ceased, as I must do at the time by means of the imagination. But though we should take away all power of imagination from the human mind, my own feelings must

leave behind them certain traces, or representations of themselves retaining the
same properties, and having the same immediate connection with the conscious
principle. On the other hand if I wish
to anticipate my own future feelings, whatever these may be, I must do so by means
of the same faculty, by which I conceive
of those of others whether past or future.
I have no distinct or separate faculty on
which the events and feelings of my future
being are impressed beforehand, and which
shews as in an inchanted mirror to me and
me alone the reversed picture of my future
life. It is absurd to suppose that the feelings which I am to have hereafter should
excite certain correspondent impressions,
or presentiments of themselves before they
exist, or act mechanically upon my mind
by a secret sympathy. I can only abstract
myself from my present being and take an
interest in my future being in the same
sense and manner, in which I can go out
of myself entirely and enter into the minds

and feelings of others. In short there neither is nor can be any principle belonging
to the individual which antecedently gives
him the same sort of connection with his
future being that he has with his past, or
that reflects the impressions of his future
feelings backwards with the same kind of
consciousness that his past feelings are
transmitted forwards through the channels
of memory. The size of the river as well
as it's taste depends on the water that has
already fallen into it. It cannot roll back
it's course, nor can the stream next the
source be affected by the water that falls
into it afterwards. Yet we call both the
same river. Such is the nature of personal
identity.* If this account be true (and

---

* Suppose a number of men employed to cast a
mound into the sea. As far as it has gone, the
workmen pass backwards and forwards on it, it
stands firm in it's place, and though it recedes
farther and farther from the shore, it is still joined
to it. A man's personal identity and self-interest
have just the same principle and extent, and can

for my own part the only perplexity that
crosses my mind in thinking of it arises from
the utter impossibility of conceiving of the
contrary supposition) it will follow that
those faculties which may be said to constitute self, and the operations of which

I 2

reach no farther than his actual existence. But if a
man of a metaphysical turn, seeing that the pier was
not yet finished, but was to be continued to a certain
point and in a certain direction, should take it into
his head to insist that what was already built and
what was to be built were the same pier, that the
one must afford as good footing as the other, and
should accordingly walk over the pier-head on the
solid foundation of his metaphysical hypothesis — he
would argue a great deal more ridiculously, but
not a whit more absurdly than those who found a
principle of absolute self-interest on a man's future
identity with his present being. But say you, the
comparison does not hold in this, that the man *can*
extend his thoughts (and that very wisely too) beyond the present moment, whereas in the other case
he cannot move a single step forwards. Grant it.
This will only shew that the mind has wings as well
as feet, which of itself is a sufficient answer to the
selfish hypothesis.

convey that idea to the mind, draw all their materials from the past and present. But all voluntary action must relate solely and exclusively to the future. That is, all those impressions or ideas with which selfish, or more properly speaking, personal feelings must be naturally connected are just those which have nothing at all to do with the motives of action.

If indeed it were possible for the human mind to alter the present or the past, so as either to recal what was done, or to give it a still greater reality, to make it exist over again and in some more emphatical sense, then man might with some pretence of reason be supposed naturally incapable of being impelled to the pursuit of any *past* or *present* object but from the mechanical excitement of personal motives. It might in this case be pretended that the impulses of imagination and sympathy are of too light, unsubstantial, and remote a nature to influence our real conduct, and that nothing is worthy of the concern of a wise

man in which he has not this direct, unavoidable, and homefelt interest. This is
however too absurd a supposition to be
dwelt on for a moment. I do not *will*
that to be which already exists as an object
of sense, nor that to have been which has
already existed, and is become an object
of memory. Neither can I will a thing
not to be which actually exists, or that which
has really existed not to have been. The
only proper objects of voluntary action are
(by necessity) future events: these can
excite no possible interest in the mind but
by means of the imagination; and these
make the same direct appeal to that faculty
whether they relate to ourselves, or others,
as the eye receives with equal directness
the impression of our own external form,
or that of others.

It will be easy to perceive in this manner how notwithstanding the contradiction
involved in the supposition of a general, absolute self-interest, the mind comes to feel
a deep and habitual conviction of the truth

of this opinion. Feeling in itself a continued consciousness of it's past impressions,
it is naturally disposed to transfer the same
sort of identity and consciousness to the
whole of it's being, as if whatever is said
generally to belong to *itself* must be inseparable from it's very existence. As our actual being is constantly passing into our
future being, and carries this internal feeling
of consciousness along with it, we seem to
be already identified with our future being
in that permanent part of our nature, and
to feel by anticipation the same sort of necessary sympathy with our future selves,
that we know we shall have with our
past selves. We take the tablets of memory, reverse them, and stamp the image
of self on that, which as yet possesses nothing but the name. It is no wonder then
that the imagination constantly outstrip-
ping the progress of time, when it's course
is marked out along the strait unbroken
line of individuality, should confound the
necessary differences of things, and confer

on my future interests a reality, and a connection with my present feelings which
they can never have. The interest which
is hereafter to be felt by this continued conscious being, this indefinite unit, called
*me*, seems necessarily to affect me in every
part of my existence. In the first place,
we abstract the successive modifications of
our being, and particular temporary interests into one simple nature, and general
principle of self-interest, and then make
use of this nominal abstraction as an artificial medium to compel those particular
actual interests into the same close affinity
and union with each other, as different
lines meeting in the same centre must have a
mutual communication with each other.—
On the other hand, as I always remain perfectly distinct from others, the interest which
I take in their past or present feelings being
(like that which I take in their future feelings)
never any thing more than the effect of
imagination and sympathy, the same illu-

sion and preposterous transposition of ideas
cannot take place with regard to them,
namely the confounding a physical impulse with the rational motives of action.
Indeed the uniform nature of my feelings
with respect to others (my interest in their
welfare having always the same source,
sympathy) seems by analogy to confirm the
supposition of a similar simplicity in my relation to myself, and of a positive, natural,
absolute interest in whatever relates to that
self, not confined to my actual existence,
but extending over the whole of my being.
Every sensation that I feel, or that afterwards recurs vividly to my memory strengthens the sense of self, which increased
strength in the mechanical feeling is transferred to the general idea, and to my remote,
future, imaginary interest: whereas our sympathy with the feelings of others being always imaginary, having no sensible interest, no restlefs mechanical impulse to urge
it on, the ties by which we are bound to
others hang loose upon us, the interest we

take in their welfare seems to be something foreign to our own bosoms, to be transient, arbitrary, and directly opposite to the necessary, absolute, permanent interest which we have in the pursuit of our own welfare.

There is however another consideration (and that the principal) to be taken into the account in explaining the origin and growth of our selfish feelings, arising out of the necessary constitution of the human mind, and not founded like the former in a mere arbitrary association of ideas. There is naturally no essential difference between the motives by which I am impelled to the pursuit of my own good and those by which I am impelled to pursue the good of others: but though there is not a difference in kind, there is one in degree. I know better what my future feelings will be than what those of others will be in the like case. I can apply the materials of memory with less difficulty and more in a mass in making out the picture of my future pleasures

and pains, without frittering them away
or destroying their original sharpnesses, in
short I can imagine them more plainly and
must therefore be more interested in them.
This facility in passing from the recollection of my past impressions to the imagination of my future ones makes the transition almost imperceptible, and gives to the
latter an apparent reality and *presentness* to
the imagination, so that the feelings of
others can never be brought home to us to
the same degree. It is chiefly from this
greater readiness and certainty with which
we can look forward into our own minds
than out of us into those of other men,
that that strong and uneasy attachment to
self which comes at last (in most minds) to
overpower every generous feeling takes it's
rise, not, as I think I have shewn, from any
natural hardness of the human heart, or
necessary absorption of all it's thoughts
and purposes in an exclusive feeling of self-
interest.

It confirms the account here given that

we always feel for others in proportion as
we know from long acquaintance what the
nature of their feelings is, and that next to
ourselves we have the strongest attachment
to our immediate relatives and friends, who
from this intercommunity of feelings and
situations may more truly be said to be a
part of ourselves than from the ties of
blood. Moreover a man must be employed more continually in providing for
his own wants and pleasures than those of
others. In like manner he is employed in
providing for the immediate welfare of his
family and connections much more than in
providing for the welfare of those, who are
not bound to him by any positive ties.
And we consequently find that the attention, time and pains bestowed on these several objects give him a proportionable degree of anxiety about, and attachment to
his own interest and that of those connected
with him, but it would be absurd to conclude that his affections are therefore cir-
cumscribed by a natural necessity within

certain limits which they cannot pass,
either in the one case, or in the other.
This general connection between the pursuit of any object and our habitual interest
in it will also account for the well-known
observation that the affection of parents to
children is the strongest of all others, frequently even overpowering self-love itself.
This fact is however inconsistent with the
supposition that the social affections are all
of them ultimately to be deduced from association, or the repeated connection of the
idea of some other person with immediate
selfish gratification. If this were the case,
we must feel the strongest attachment to
those from whom we had received, instead
of those to whom we had done the greatest
number of kindnesses, or where the greatest
quantity of selfish enjoyment had been associated with an indifferent idea. Junius
has remarked, that friendship is not conci-
liated " by the power of conferring bene-
fits, but the equality with which they are
received, and may be returned."

I have hitherto purposely avoided saying any thing on the subject of our physical appetites, and the manner in which they may be thought to affect the principle of the foregoing reasonings. They evidently seem at first sight to contradict the general conclusion which I have endeavoured to establish, as they all of the mtend either exclusively or principally to the gratification of the individual, and at the same time refer to some future or imaginary object as the source of this gratification. The impulse which they give to the will is mechanical, and yet this impulse, blind as it is, constantly tends to, and coalesces with the pursuit of some rational end. That is, here is an end aimed at, the desire and regular pursuit of a known good, and all this produced by motives evidently mechanical, and which never impel the mind but in a selfish direction. It makes no difference in the question whether the active impulse proceeds directly from the desire of positive enjoyment, or a wish to get rid of some

positive uneasiness. I should say then
that setting aside what is of a purely physical, or (for aught I can tell) instinctive nature in the case, the influence of appetite
over our volitions may be accounted for
consistently enough with the foregoing hypothesis from the natural effects of a particularly irritable state of bodily feeling, ren-
dering the idea of that which will heighten
and gratify it's susceptibility of pleasurable
feeling, or remove some painful feeling pro-
portionably vivid, and the object of a more
vehement desire than can be excited by the
same idea, when the body is supposed to
be in a state of indifference, or only ordi-
nary sensibility to that particular kind of
gratification. Thus the imaginary desire
is sharpened by constantly receiving fresh
supplies of pungency from the irritation
of bodily feeling, and it's direction is at the
same time determined according to the bias
of this new impulse, first indirectly by
having the attention fixed on our own immediate sensations; secondly, because that

particular gratification, the desire of which is increased by the pressure of physical appetite, must be referred primarily and by way of distinction to the same being, by whom the want of it is felt, that is, to myself. As the actual uneasiness which appetite implies can only be excited by the irritable state of my own body, so neither can the desire of the correspondent gratification subsist in that intense degree which properly constitutes appetite, except when it tends to relieve that very same uneasiness by which it was excited. As in the case of hunger. There is in the first place the strong mechanical action of the nervous and muscular systems co-operating with the rational desire of my own relief, and forcing it it's own way. Secondly, this state of uneasiness continues to grow more and more violent, the longer the relief which it requires is withheld from it:—hunger takes no denial, it hearkens to no compromise, is soothed by no flattery, tired out by no delay. It grows more importunate

every moment, it's demands become louder
the less they are attended to. The first
impulse which the general love of personal
ease receives from bodily pain will give it
the advantage over my disposition to sympathize with others in the same situation
with myself; and this difference will be in-
creasing every moment, till the pain is removed. Thus if I at first either through
compassion or by an effort of the will am
regardless of my own wants, and wholly
bent upon satisfying the more pressing
wants of my companions, yet this effort
will at length become too great, and I shall
be incapable of attending to any thing but
the violence of my own sensations, or the
means of alleviating them. It is plain with
respect to one of our appetites, I mean the
sexual, where the gratification of the same
passion in another is the means of gratify-
ing our own, that our physical sensibility
stimulates our sympathy with the desires of
the other sex, and on the other hand this
feeling of mutual sympathy increases the

physical desires of both. This is indeed the chief foundation of the sexual passion, though I believe that it's immediate and determining cause depends upon other principles not to be here lightly touched on *. It would be easy to shew from many things that mere appetite (generally at least in reasonable beings) is but the fragment of a self-moving machine, but a sort of half-organ, a subordinate instrument even in the accomplishment of it's own purposes; that it does little or nothing without the aid of another faculty to inform and direct it. There are several striking examples of this given by Rousseau in relating the progress of his own passions. (See the first volume of his Confessions.) Before the impulses of appetite can be converted into the regular pursuit of a given object, they must first be communicated to the understanding, and modify the will through that. Consequently as the desire of the ultimate gra-

* See Preface to Wordsworth's Poems,

K

tification of the appetite is not the same
with the appetite itself, that is mere physical uneasiness, but an indirect result
of its communication to the thinking or
imaginative principle, the influence of appetite over the will must depend on the extraordinary degree of force and vividness
which it gives to the idea of a particular object; and accordingly we find that the same
cause, which irritates the desire of selfish
gratification, increases our sensibility to
the same desires and gratification in others,
where they are consistent with our own,
and where the violence of the physical impulse does not overpower every other consideration.

Make the most of the objection,—it can
only apply to the determinations of the will
while it is subject to the gross influence of
another faculty, with which it has neither
the same natural direction, nor is it in general at all controuled by it. The question which I have proposed to examine is
whether there is any general principle of

selfishness in the human mind, or whether
it is not naturally disinterested. Now the effects of appetite are so far from being any
confirmation of the first supposition, that
we are even oftener betrayed by them into
actions contrary to our own well-known,
clear, and lasting interest than into those
which are injurious to others. The
" short-lived pleasure" and the " lasting
woe" fall to the lot of the same being.——I
will give one more example and then have
done. A man addicted to the pleasures
of the bottle is less able to govern this propensity after drinking a certain quantity
and feeling the actual pleasure and state of
excitement which it produces, than he is
to abstain entirely from it's indulgence.
When once the liquor *gets into his head,* to
use the common phrase, the force which
it gives to his predominant feeling gets the
better of every other idea, and he from
that time loses all power of self-controul.
Both before, and after this, however, the
same feeling of actual excitement, which

urges him on, makes him enter more cordially into the convivial dispositions of his companions, and a man is always earnest that others should drink as he becomes unwilling to desist himself.

To add that there is but one instance in which appetite hangs about a man as a perpetual clog and dead-weight upon the reason, namely the sexual appetite, and that here the selfish habit produced by this constant state of animal sensibility seems to have a direct counterpoise given to it by nature in the mutual sympathy of the sexes. Quere also whether this general susceptibility is not itself an effect of an irritable imagination exerted on that particular subject. (See Notes to the Essay on the Inequality of Mankind.) I hope this will be sufficient to break the force of the objection as above stated, and may perhaps furnish a clue to a satisfactory account of the subject itself.

I do not think I should illustrate the foregoing reasoning so well by any thing I could add on the subject as by relating the manner in which it first struck me.—There are moments in the life of a solitary thinker which are to him what the evening of some great victory is to the conqueror and hero—milder triumphs long remembered with truer and deeper delight. And though the shouts of multitudes do not hail his success, though gay trophies, though the sounds of music, the glittering of armour, and the neighing of steeds do not mingle with his joy, yet shall he not want monuments and witnesses of his glory, the deep forest, the willowy brook, the gathering clouds of winter, or the silent gloom of his own chamber, " faithful remembrancers of his high endeavour, and his glad success," that, as time passes by him with unreturning wing, still awaken the consciousness of a spirit patient, indefatigable in the search of truth, and the hope of surviving in the thoughts and minds of other men.—I remember I had been reading a speech which Mirabeau

(the author of the System of Nature) has
put into the mouth of a supposed atheist
at the Last Judgment; and was afterwards
led on by some means or other to consider
the question whether it could properly be
said to be an act of virtue in any one to
sacrifice his own final happiness to that of
any other person or number of persons, if
it were possible for the one ever to be made
the price of the other. Suppose it were
my own case—that it were in my power to
save twenty other persons by voluntarily
consenting to suffer for them: why should
I not do a generous thing, and never trouble myself about what might be the consequence to myself the Lord knows when?—
The reason why a man should prefer his
own future welfare to that of others is that
he has a necessary, absolute interest in the
one which he cannot have in the other, and
this again is a consequence of his being always the same individual, of his continued
identity with himself. The difference I
thought was this, that however insensible I

may be to my own interest at any future
period, yet when the time comes I shall feel
differently about it. I shall then judge of
it from the actual impression of the object,
that is truly and certainly; and as I shall
still be conscious of my past feelings and
shall bitterly regret my own folly and insensibility, I ought as a rational agent
to be determined now by what I shall then
wish I had done when I shall feel the consequences of my actions most deeply and
sensibly. It is this continued consciousness of my own feelings which gives me an
immediate interest in whatever relates to
my future welfare, and makes me at all
times accountable to myself for my own
conduct. As therefore this consciousness
will be renewed in me after death, if I exist again at all—But stop—As I must be
conscious of my past feelings to be myself,
and as this conscious being will be myself,
how if that consciousness should be transferred to some other being? How am I to
know that I am not imposed upon by a

false claim of identity ?—But that is ridiculous because you will have no other self
than that which arises from this very consciousness. Why then this self may be
multiplied in as many different beings as
the Deity may think proper to endue with
the same consciousness, which if it can be
renewed at will in any one instance, may
clearly be so in an hundred others. Am I
to regard all these as equally myself? Am
I equally interested in the fate of all? Or
if I must fix upon some one of them in
particular as my representative and other
self, how am I to be determined in my
choice ?—Here then I saw an end put to
my speculations about absolute self-interest,
and personal identity. I saw plainly that
the consciousness of my own feelings which
is made the foundation of my continued
interest in them could not extend to what
had never been, and might never be, that
my identity with myself must be confined
to the connection between my past and
present being, that with respect to my fu-

ture feelings or interests they could have no communication with, or influence over my present feelings and interests merely because they were future, that I shall be hereafter affected by the recollection of my past feelings and actions, and my remorse be equally heightened by reflecting on my past folly and late-earned wisdom whether I am really the same being, or have only the same consciousness renewed in me, but that to suppose that this remorse can react in the reverse order on my present feelings, or give me an immediate interest in my future feelings, before it exists, is an express contradiction in terms. It can only affect me as an imaginary idea, or an idea of truth. But so may the interests of others; and the question proposed was whether I have not some real, necessary, absolute interest in whatever relates to my future being in consequence of my immediate connection with myself, independently of the general impression which all positive ideas have on my mind. How then can

this pretended unity of consciousness
which is only reflected from the past,
which makes me so little acquainted with
the future that I cannot even tell for a
moment how long it will be continued,
whether it will be entirely interrupted by or
renewed in me after death, and which might
be multiplied in I don't know how many
different beings and prolonged by complicated sufferings without my being any
the wiser for it, how I say can a principle
of this sort identify my present with my
future interests, and make me as much a
a participater in what does not at all affect me as if it were actually impressed
on my senses? It is plain as this conscious being may be decompounded, entirely destroyed, renewed again, or multiplied in a great number of beings, and
as, whichever of these takes place, it cannot produce the least alteration in my
present being, that what I am does not
depend on what I am to be, and that
there is no communication between my

future interests, and the motives by which my present conduct must be governed. This can no more be influenced by what may be my future feelings with respect to it than it will then be possible for me to alter my past conduct by wishing that I had acted differently. I cannot therefore have a principle of active self-interest arising out of the immediate connection between my present and future self, for no such connection exists, or is possible. I am what I am in spite of the future. My feelings, actions, and interests must be determined by causes already existing and acting, and are absolutely independent of the future. Where there is not an intercommunity of feelings, there can be no identity of interests. My personal interest in any thing must refer either to the interest excited by the actual impression of the object which cannot be felt before it exists, and can last no longer than while the impression lasts, or it may refer to the particular manner in

which I am mechanically affected by the *idea*
of my own impressions in the absence of the
object. I can therefore have no proper
personal interest in my future impressions, since neither my ideas of future objects, nor my feelings with respect to them
can be excited either directly or indirectly by
the impressions themselves or by any ideas
or feelings accompanying them without a
complete transposition of the order in
which effects follow one another in nature.——The only reason for my preferring my
future interest to that of others must arise
from my anticipating it with greater warmth
of present imagination. It is this greater
liveliness and force with which I can enter into my future feelings, that in a manner
identifies them with my present being;
and this notion of identity being once
formed, the mind makes use of it to
strengthen it's habitual propensity, by giving to personal motives a reality and absolute truth which they can never have.
Hence it has been inferred that my real, sub-

stantial interest in any thing must be derived
in some indirect manner from the impression
of the object itself, as if that could have
any sort of communication with my present feelings, or excite any interest in my
mind but by means of the imagination,
which is naturally affected in a certain
manner by the prospect of future good or
evil.

# REMARKS

ON

## THE SYSTEMS OF

## HARTLEY AND HELVETIUS.

I FIND I owe the reader two explanations, one relating to the association of ideas, from which Hartley and other writers have deduced the origin of all our affections, even of self-love itself, the other relating to the mechanical principle of self-interest stated by Helvetius.* It was my first in-

* I do not mean that Helvetius was the first who conceived the hypothesis here spoken of (for I do not think he had wit enough to invent even an ingenious absurdity) but it was through him I believe that this notion has obtained it's present popularity, and in France particularly it has had, I am certain, a very general influence on the national character. It was brought forward in the most forcible manner by the writers of the last century, and it is expressly stated, and clearly answered by Bishop Butler in the Preface to his Sermons at the Rolls' Chapel. After Berkeley's Essay on Vision, I do

tention to have given at the end of the preceding essay a general account of the nature of the will, and to have tried at least to dig down a little deeper into the foundation of human thoughts and actions than I have hitherto done. At present I have laid aside all thoughts of this kind as I have neither time nor strength for such an undertaking; and the most that I shall attempt is to point out such contradictions and difficulties in both these systems as may lessen the weight of any objections drawn from them against the one I have stated, and leave the argument as above explained in it's original force.

To begin with the doctrine of association.

The general principle of association as laid down by Hartley is this, that if any given sensation, idea, or motion be for a number of times either accompanied, or immediately followed by any other sensa-

not know of any work better worth the attention of those who would learn to think than these same metaphysical Discourses preached at the Rolls' Chapel.

tion, idea, or muscular motion, the recurrence of the one will afterwards mechanically give rise to that of the other. By *immediately followed* I mean *closely followed*: for suppose A to be associated with B, and B with C,
A will not only produce B and C intermedi-
ately, but will in time produce C immediately without the intervention of B. A
mathematician would perhaps here ask how
this can ever be actually proved : for
though it seems reasonable to suppose that
the influence of A if it extend to B should
also go a little farther to the next idea, and
join indirectly and secretly with B in producing C, yet as the connection between
A and B must be stronger than that between A and C, if in any case the connection between the former become gradually so
weakened as to dissolve of itself, the latter
must fail of course, and therefore C can
never follow A, except when B stands
equivocally between them. This question
would go upon the supposition, that B

L

and C must always be impressions of exactly the same kind and degree of strength
which is not the case. A, though more remote from C, may yet be more intimately
connected with it than with B from several
other causes, from the greater strength
of the impression, from similarity, &c.
(This implies by the bye that the effect of
association depends on the conjunction of
many circumstances, and principles of action, and is not simply determined by the
relation of proximity or remoteness between our ideas with respect to time or
place.) Thus if a person has done a number of good actions, which have been ob-
served with pleasure by another, this ap-
probation will be afterwards associated
with the idea of the person, and the recollection of the benevolent disposition which
gave birth to those actions remains when
the particular manner in which it was exerted is forgotten. First, because the feeling is the principal or strongest circumstance.

Secondly, the association of our ideas with moral qualities is evidently assisted, and forced into the same general direction by the simplicity and uniform character of our feelings compared with the great variety of things and actions, which makes it impossible to combine such a number of distinct forms under the same general notion.

What I have here stated is I believe the whole extent and compass of the law of association. It has been said that this principle is of itself sufficient to account for all the phenomena of the human mind, and is the foundation of every rule of morality. My design is to shew that both these assertions are absolutely false, or that it is an absurdity, and an express contradiction to suppose that association is either the only mode of operation of the human mind, or that it is the primary and most general principle of thought and action.—But first of all it will be necessary to consider the account which Hartley himself has given of

this principle as depending on the mechanical communication of motion from the
seat of one idea to that of the next and so
on, according to a certain local arrangement of these ideas in the brain, as certainly if thought is carried on in this manner, that is, by means of vibrations, it is
difficult to conceive of it's being produced
by any other means than the accidental
justling of these one against the other,
which is what is meant by association.

There are two or three general observations which will be of use in conducting us
through this inquiry. In the first place
it appears to me certain that every impression or idea is produced in such a manner
as to affect or be perceived by the whole
brain at once, or in immediate succession,
that is, before the action ceases. For if
we suppose a certain degree of resemblance
to subsist between two ideas, the perception of the one will always be sure to excite a recollection of the other, if it is at

all worth remembering. I mean for instance if a person should in some strange
place suddenly see an excellent picture
of their dead father or mother, I suppose there can be no doubt but the picture would call up the memory of the person whom it resembled with an instantane-
ous and irresistible force. Now this could
not always happen but on the supposition
that the visible impression of the picture
was conveyed to every part of the brain,
as otherwise it must be a mere accident
whether it would ever come in contact
with that part of it, where that distinct set
of recollections was lodged which it was
calculated to excite. It is evident that
the force with which the impression of the
picture acts upon the mind is subsequent
to the recollection of the likeness and not
the cause of it, since the picture of any
other person would act physically upon my
mind in the same manner. It may be
worth remarking here that the strength, or
habitual or recent recurrence of any idea

makes it more easily recollected. I might
see a picture of a person whom I had not
often seen and whose face did not at all interest me at the time without recollecting
whose it was, though the likeness should
be never so great. The frequent recurrence of the imitation on the other hand
if it has had it's usual effect renders the
recollection of the object less certain or at
any rate less vivid every time, till at last
what remains of it is entirely lost, and confounded with the imitation *. Again, it
is also certain that the proximity of the
parts of an object to one another, or of
one object to another object is of itself a
sufficient and necessary reason for their recollection in succession or together, in the same
order in which they were actually perceived.
Unless this were the case, we could never
recollect any thing at all, as every object

* No doubt the picture is always looked at with
a very different feeling from what it would have
been, if the idea of the person had never been distinctly associated with it.

is necessarily composed of parts, and those again of others without end. Now how are we to reconcile this with the first-mention inference that thought is uniformly and necessarily communicated to every part of the thinking substance? If thought is produced in such a manner, that the shock is immediately felt in those parts nearest the seat of the individual impression, and is indeed sure to excite thought in them without ever affecting the remote parts of the brain in the same manner, it seems strange that it's own communication over the whole brain should be so rapid and certain, while the force with which it is sent along (as implied in it's confined power of producing other thoughts by simple impulse) is so unequal.

The reader will I hope have the good-nature to pardon some inconsistencies of expression in treating of this subject. In order to disprove the theory which I am combating I must first assume it's truth, and go on talking of *the seats of our ideas*, *the different parts of the brain, the commu-nication of thought by impulse,* &c. till it is clearly shewn that the hypothesis to which all these expressions refer is in reality good for nothing.

Though I do not see my way out of the dilemma here stated, and find I have engaged in an undertaking I am not equal to, I think I have seen enough of the difficul-ties belonging to it to be able to reject the Hartleian hypothesis as directly incompa-tible with a fair and comprehensive view of the subject. For, first, it has been shewn above that every idea, or perception is communicated to all the parts of the brain, or to the whole sentient principle, whatever this is supposed to be. Or the same thing might be shewn from the nature of consci-ousness *. That there is some faculty of

---

* Consciousness is here and all along (where any particular stress is laid upon it) used in it's etymo-logical sense, as literally the same with *conscientia*, the knowing or perceiving many things by a simple act.

this sort which opens a direct communication between our ideas, so that the same thinking principle is at the same time conscious of different impressions, and of their relations to each other, is what hardly any person who attends in the least to what passes in his own mind and is not determined to reason himself out of his senses will I should think deny. In other words, when any two ideas or parts of an idea (for there is no difference in this respect) as those of two lighted candles, or the top and bottom of the same candle are impressed at the same time on different parts of the brain, before these ideas can be perceived in connection as making parts of a whole, or can be accompanied with a consciousness of each other's existence, we must suppose them mutually to affect the seats of action belonging to each other, or else to be united in some common principle of thought, the same comparing power being exerted upon both. Without supposing their distinct impressions thus to meet in

the same point, it seems a thing impossible
to conceive how any comparison can take
place between different impressions existing at the same time, or between our past,
and present impressions, or ever to explain
what is meant by saying, *I perceive such
and such objects, I remember such and such
events,* since these different impressions are
evidently referred to the same conscious being, which idea of individuality could
never have been so much as conceived of
if there were no other connection between
our ideas than that which arises from the
juxtaposition of the particles of matter on
which they are severally impressed. The
mere juxtaposition of the parts of the thinking substance on which different ideas are
impressed will never produce any thing
more than the actual juxtaposition of the
ideas themselves, unaccompanied by any
consciousness of their having this relation
to each other: for the mind in this case
consisting of nothing more than a succession of material points, each part will be

sensible of the corresponding part of any object which is impressed upon it, but can know nothing of the impression which is made on any other part of the same substance, except from it's reaction on the seat of the first, which is contrary to the supposition. In short, to attempt accounting at all for the nature of consciousness from the proximity of different impressions, or of their fluxional parts to each other in the brain seems no less absurd than it would be to imagine that by placing a number of persons together in a line we should produce in them an immediate consciousness and perfect knowledge of what was passing in each other's minds. If consciousness is to be deduced at all from the circumstance of place, it must be that different impressions occupy exactly the same place. One place has no identity with another: however thin the partition between one idea and another, the distinction must be as absolute and complete, and must confine each idea as effectually within it's own bounds in this fantastical mosaic-work of the brain, as if the solid skulls of ten philosophers were interposed between each. There is another consideration to be attended to, which is that sensible impressions appear to be continually made on the same part of the brain in succession:—with respect to those received by the eye, a new set of objects is almost every moment impressed on the whole organ, and consequently transmitted along the nerves to the same receptacle in the brain*. It follows from this last observation in particular (which is not a speculative refinement but a plain matter of fact) that the sphere occupied by

* Those of the touch admit of the greatest variety in this respect from the general diffusion of that sense over the whole body, and those which depend on hearing from the small part of the ear which is in general distinctly affected by sound at the same time. As to the taste and smell, the stimulants applied to these senses are such as for the most part to act on a large proportion of the organ at once, though only at intervals. The direction of smells is hardly distinquishable like that of sounds.

different vibrations is constantly the same, or that the same region of the brain belongs equally to a thousand different impressions, and consequently that the mere circumstance of situation is insufficient to account for that complete distinctness, of which our ideas are capable.

From all these considerations taken together I cannot help inferring the fallacy of the Hartleian doctrine of vibrations, which all along goes on the supposition of the most exact distinction and regular arrangement of the *places* of our ideas, and which therefore cannot be effectually reconciled with any reasoning that excludes all local distinction from having a share in the mechanical operations of the human mind. For if we suppose the succession of our ideas to be carried on by the communication of the impulse belonging to one idea to the contiguous cell, or dormitory of another idea formerly associated with it, and if we at the same time suppose each idea to occupy a separate cell which is inviolable,

and which it has entirely to itself, then un-
doubtedly the ideas thus called up will follow one another in the same order in which
they were originally excited. But if we
take away this imaginary allotment of separate parcels of the brain to different ideas
and suppose the same substance or principle to be constantly impressed with a succession of different ideas, then there seems
to be no assignable reason why a vibratory
motion accompanied with thought in passing from one part of the thinking substance
to the next should not excite any other idea
which had been impressed there, as well as
the one with which that particular vibration had been originally associated, or why
it should not by one general impulse
equally excite them all. It is like supposing that you might tread on a nest of
adders twined together, and provoke only
one of them to sting you. On the other
hand to say that this species of elective affinity
is determined in it's operation by the greater
readiness with which the idea of a particu-

lar impression recalls the memory of another
impression which co-existed with it in a
state of sensible excitement is to repeat the
fact but not (that I can perceive) in any
manner to account for it. Let any one
compare this account with the one given
by Hartley of his own principle, and he
will be able to judge.

But farther, even if it could be shewn that
the doctrine of vibrations accounts satisfactorily for the association of the ideas of any
one sense, (as those of the sight for example) yet surely the very nature of that
principle must cut off every sort of communication between the ideas of different
senses, (as those of sight and hearing) which
may have been associated in the order of
time, but which with respect to actual situation must be farther removed from one
another than any ideas of the same sense,
at whatever distance of time they may
have been severally impressed. If from
the top of a long cold barren hill I hear
the distant whistle of a thrush which seems

to come up from some warm woody shelter beyond the edge of the hill, this sound coming faint over the rocks with a mingled feeling of strangeness and joy, the idea of the place about me, and the imaginary one beyond will all be combined together in such a manner in my mind as to become inseparable. Now the doctrine of vibrations appears absolutely to exclude the possibility of the union of all these into one *associated* idea, because as the whole of that principle is founded on the greater ease and certainty with which one local impression is supposed to pass into the seat of the next, and the greater force with which it acts there than it can do farther off, the idea of a visible object can never run into the notion of a sound, nor *vice versâ*, these impressions being of course conveyed along different nerves to different and very remote parts of the brain. Perhaps it will be said that all ideas impressed at the same moment of time may be supposed to be assigned to particular compartments of the

brain as well as where the external objects
are contiguous. To this I should answer
that such a supposition does not at all account for what I have said above with respect to consciousness and the association
of ideas from similarity, &c. and secondly,
this supposition is neither included in
Hartley's theory, nor does it seem to be
compatible with it, as there is no other
reason on the common material hypothesis
for inferring the contiguity of our ideas in
the brain than the contiguity of their external objects, and the impression of those
objects on corresponding parts of the external sensible organ.

The whole of Hartley's system is founded
on what seems an entirely gratuitous supposition, viz. the imaginary communication of our ideas to particular places in
the brain to correspond not only with the
relations of external objects, but with the
order of time. This supposition can never
be reconciled with the inference mentioned
above (to go no farther) that thought is

communicated to every part of the thinking substance by an immediate and uniform
impulse.    For though we should suppose
that it is communicated in one manner to
what may be called it's *primary seat*, and
in a different manner over the rest of the
brain, yet we shall still be as much at a
loss as ever to  shew a reason why it's primary action should always excite the associated or  contiguous ideas, while it's indirect or secondary action has no power at
all to excite any of the ideas, with the
spheres of which it necessarily comes in
contact in it's general diffusion over the
whole brain, that is by it's simple impulse.
This is not all.    There is another circumstance which must entirely prevent the
least use being made of this distinction,
which is that associated ideas are not properly such as are contiguous in place, but
all such as are connected in point of time,
the relation of place not being at all essential in the question, for ideas that have
been impressed together are always recol-

lected as parts of the same complex impression, without any regard to the proximity or remoteness of their direct, primary seats in the brain, considered as distinct local impressions. As has been explained above with respect to sounds and visible objects, where the association must evidently arise fr omwhat I have called their secondary, or relative actions, or, if you will, their *conscious ideas*, that is those which are not confined to a particular spot in the circumference of the brain, but affect the general principle of thought, whatever this may be, whether composed of extended, material parts, or indivisible. Now if these secondary or conscious ideas which we may represent as continually posting backwards and forwards like couriers in all directions through all quarters of the brain to meet each other and exchange accounts are in fact the only instruments of association, it is plain that the account given by Hartley of that principle falls to the ground at once, first because that account affords no explanation of any of the associations which take place in the mind, except when there is an immediate communication between the primary seats of the associated ideas; secondly, because these secondary or conscious ideas being spread over the whole brain, or rather being impressed on the same thinking principle cannot have any particular connection with or power to call up one another or the contrary from any circumstances of local distinction, which is thus completely done away.—The doctrine of vibrations supposes the order of place and the order of time to correspond exactly in all combinations of our ideas, and that it is owing to this circumstance entirely that those ideas which have been impressed nearly at the same time have afterwards a power to call up one another from the facility with which they must be supposed to pass from their own primary seats into the contiguous ones of the associated ideas. I have endeavoured to shew on the contrary not only that there is no regular local arrangement of our ideas to correspond exactly with the order in which they cohere together in the mind, but that there appears to be no distinction whatever in this respect, that they all belong absolutely to the same place or internal seat of consciousness, that this want of distinction is an evident fact with respect to the successive impressions which are made on the same parts of the body, and consequently on the same parts of the thinking substance, and that it may be deduced generally from the nature of thought itself, and the associations which arise from similarity, &c. that this principle must be entirely nugatory with respect to the associations of the ideas of different senses, even though it should hold true with respect to those of any one sense*, lastly that

* The method taken by Hartley in detailing the associations, which take place between the ideas of each of the senses one by one, saves him the trouble of explaining those which take place between the ideas of different senses at the same time.

all ideas impressed at the same time acquire a power of exciting one another ever after without any regard to the coincidence of their imaginary seats in the brain (according to the material hypothesis) and that therefore the true account of the principle of association must be derived from the first cause, viz. the coincidence of time, and not from the latter which bears no manner of proportion to the effects produced.

The account indeed which Hartley has in one place given of successive association as distinct from synchronous seems to have no necessary connection with this last-mentioned principle. He says, page 69, " If A and B be vibrations impressed suc-" cessively, then will the latter part of A, " viz. that part which remains after the " impression of the object ceases, be mo-" dified and altered by B, at the same time " that it will a little modify and alter it, till " at last it be quite overpowered by it, and " end in it. It follows therefore that the

" successive impression of A and B suffi-
" ciently repeated will so alter the medul-
" lary substance, as that when A is im-
" pressed alone, it's latter part shall not
" be such as the sole impression of A re-
" quires, but lean towards B, and end in
" *c* at last. But B will not excite *a* in a
" retrograde order, since, by supposition.
" the latter part of B was not modified
" and altered by A, but by some other vi-
" bration, such as C or D." First of all,
this account seems to imply that the associated impressions A and B are the only
ones made on the mind, and that they extend over the whole medullary substance.
In this case when the action of A ceases or
grows very weak, we may suppose that
the tendency to B will be gradually re-
vived, and at last completely overpower
that of A. because these are the only impressions existing in the mind, and it must
consequently incline to one or other of
them, which would be equally the case,
whether they had been impressed together

or not. Otherwise we must suppose the impressions thus made successively to have a distinct local communication with each other, or there is no reason given why A should excite *b* more than any other vibration impressed on the brain in general, or on the seat of *b* in particular. We must besides this suppose the vibrations A and B to have a particular line of direction, as well as primary sphere of action in the brain to account for B's not exciting *a* in the reverse order, &c. The question is how the impression of different objects at the same time, or in quick succession gives the idea of one of those objects a power to excite the idea of the other, though the object is absent; and it is no answer to this question to say, that A being often repeated in connection with B, when it is afterwards excited, " leans towards B, and ends in it." Hartley says by way of breaking the difficulty, that the latter part of A is altered and modified by B. This is evident enough while B really acts upon the senses : but why should it be modified by it in the absence of B ? This modification of the latter part of A by B is not the intermediate cause of the excitement of $b$, for $b$, the representative of B, must be excited, at least imperfectly, before it can modify A (B itself being nothing) and the point is how A, or $a$ excites the movement connected with B and that only, not how, supposing this connection between them to be established, the one gradually passes into the other, and ends in it. I think Hartley constantly mistakes tracing the order of palpable effects, or overt acts of the mind for explaining the causes of the connection between them, which he hardly ever does with a true metaphysical feeling. Even where he is greatest, he is always the physiologist rather than the metaphysician *.

* I have always had the same feeling with respect to Hartley (still granting his power to the utmost) which is pleasantly expressed in an old author, Roger Bacon, quoted by Sir Kenelm Digby in his

Perhaps a better way to set about discovering the clue to the principle of asso-

answer to Brown. " Those students" he says, " who busy themselves much with such notions as " relate wholly to the fantasie, do hardly ever be-" come idoneous for abstracted metaphysical specu-" lations; the one having bulky foundation of mat-" ter or of the accidents of it to settle upon, (at the " least with one foot :) the other flying continually, " even to a lessening pitch, in the subtil air. And " accordingly, it hath been generally noted, that " the exactest mathematicians, who converse altoge-" ther with lines, figures, and other differences of " quantity, have seldom proved eminent in meta-" physicks or speculative divinity. Nor again, the " professors of these sciences in the other arts. " Much less can it be expected, that an excellent " physician, whose fancy is always fraught with the " material drugs that he prescribeth his apothecary " to compound his medicines of, and whose hands " are inured to the cutting up, and eyes to the in-" spection of anatomized bodies, should easily and " with success, flie his thoughts at so towring a " game, as a pure intellect, a separated and unbo-" died soul."—I confess I feel in reading Hartley something in the way in which the Dryads must

ciation, setting aside all ideas of extension,
contiguity, &c. would be by considering

have done shut up in their old oak trees. I feel my
sides pressed hard, and bored with points of knotty
inferences piled up one upon another without being
able ever to recollect myself, or catch a glimpse of
the actual world without me. I am somehow
wedged in between different rows of material objects,
overpowering me by their throng, and from which
I have no power to escape, but of which I neither
know nor understand any thing. I constantly see
objects multiplied upon me, not powers at work, I
know no reason why one thing follows another but
that something else is conjured up between them, which
has as little apparent connection with either as they
have with one another ;—he always reasons from the
concrete object, not from the abstract or essential
properties of things, and in his whole book I do not
believe that there is one good definition. It would
be a bad way to describe a man's character to say
that he had a wise father or a foolish son, and yet
this is the way in which Hartley defines ideas by
stating what precedes them in the mind, and what
comes after them. Thus he defines the will to be
" that idea, or *state of mind* which precedes action,"
or " a desire, or aversion sufficiently strong to pro-
" duce action," &c. He gives you the outward

the manner in which the same conscious
principle may be supposed to adapt itself
to, to combine, and as it were reconcile
together the actions of different objects impressed on it at once, and to all of which
it is forced to attend at the same time; by
which means these several impressions thus
compelled into agreement, and a kind of
mutual understanding one with another
afterwards retain a particular tendency or
disposition to unite together, that is to say,
the mind when thrown back into the same
state by the recurrence of any one of these
ideas is of course put into the way of admitting or passing more readily to any
other of the same set of ideas than to any
other ideas of a different set not so blended
and harmonized with it. It seems as if

signs of things in the order in which he conceives
them to follow one another, never the demonstration
of certain consequences from the known nature of their
causes, which alone is true reasoning. Nevertheless,
it is not to be forgotten, that he was also a great
man. See his Chapter on Memory, &c.

the mind was laid open to all the impressions which had been made upon it at any given time, the moment any one of them recalls a state of feeling habitually in unison with the rest. By touching a certain spring, all obstacles are removed, the doors fly open, and the whole gallery is seen at a single glance.—The mind has a capacity to perform any complex action the easier for having performed the same action before. It will consequently have a disposition to perform that action rather than any other, the other circumstances being the same. I imagine that association is to be accounted for on the very same principle as a man's being able to comprehend or *take in* a mathematical demonstration the better for going over it a number of times, or to recognise any well-known object, as the figure of a man for instance in the middle of a common, sooner than a stump of a tree, or piece of a rock of twice the size, and of just as remarkable a shape.—In like manner, or at least consis-

tently with this, we may suppose, if one
impression is very like another, though not
*associated* with it, that the mind will in
that case slide more naturally, will feel
less repugnance in passing from the recollection of the one to that of the other, that
is from it's actual state into a state very
little different from it than into one of a
totally different kind. When any particular idea becomes predominant, the turn
which is thus given to the mind must be
favourable to the reception or recollection
of any other idea, which requires but little alteration in the state of the mind to admit it. A slight turn of the screws on
which the tension of the mind depends will
set it right to the point required. When
the actual state of the mind agrees, or falls
in with some previous tendency, the effort
which the latent idea makes to pass into a
state of excitement must be more powerful
than it would be without this co-opera-
tion, and where the other circumstances
are indifferent must always be effectual.

Thus the actual feeling of warmth must
have a tendency to call up any old ideas
of the same kind: *e. g.* to-day being a
very warm day put me in mind of a walk
I took in a hot day last summer. Here
however another difficulty occurs: for the
very opposition of our feelings as of heat
and cold frequently produces a transition
in the mind from the one to the other.
This may be accounted for in a loose way
by supposing, that the struggle between
very opposite feelings producing a violent and perturbed state of mind excites
attention, and makes the mind more sensible to the shock of the contrary impression to that by which it is preoccupied,
as we find that the body is more liable to
be affected by any opposite extremes, as of
heat and cold, immediately succeeding,
and counteracting each other. Be this as
it may, all things naturally put us in mind
of their contraries, cold of heat, day of
night, &c. These three, viz. association,
similarity, and contrast I believe include

all the general sources of connection between our ideas, for as to that of cause and
effect, it seems to be referable (as remarked
by Priestley) or at least chiefly so to the first
class, that of common association.—I hope
no one will think me weak enough to imagine that what I have here stated is even a
remote and faint approach to a satisfactory
account of the matter. Every attempt of
this sort must be light and ineffectual without first ascertaining (if that were possible)
the manner in which our ideas are produced, and the nature of consciousness,
both of which I am utterly unable to comprehend. I have endeavoured simply to
point out what it is that is to be accounted
for, the general feeling with which a reflecting man should set out in search of the truth,
and the impossibility of ever ariving at it,
if at the outset we completely cover over
our own feelings with maps of the brain,
dry skulls, musical chords, pendulums,
and compasses, or think of looking into
the bottom of our own minds by means of

any other instrument than a sharpened intellect.

What I at first proposed was to shew, that association, however we may suppose it to be carried on, is not the only source of connection between our ideas, or mode of operation of the human mind. This has been assumed indirectly, and I think proved with respect to similarity, &c. Here however a shrewd turn has been given to the argument by the Hartleians, who, admitting similarity among the causes of connection between our ideas, deny that it is any objection to their doctrine, for that this very example is easily resolved into a case of mere association. Similarity they say is nothing but partial sameness, and that where part of a thing has been first associated with certain circumstances, and is afterwards conjoined with others, making in fact two different objects, it's recurrence in the second instance will necessarily recall the circumstances with which

N

it was associated in the first *.——In general
we suppose that if we meet a person in the
street with a face resembling some other
face with which we are well acquainted,
the reason why the one puts us in mind of
the other is *that the one is like the other ;* and
we should be little disposed to believe any
one who told us seriously that in reality we
had before seen the one man's nose upon
the other's face, and that this old impression or very identical object brought
along with it the other ideas with which
it had been formerly associated. This
account would be sufficiently contrary
to common sense and feeling, and I
hope to shew that it has as little connection with any true subtlety of thinking.
No metaphysician will I am sure be disposed to controvert this, who takes the
trouble accurately to compare the meaning
of the explanation with the terms and necessary import of the law of association.
For let an impression which I received yes-

* See Priestley's Letters to a Philosophical Un-
believer.

terday be in every possible respect the
same with the one which I received to-day,
still the one impression is not the other;
they are two distinct impressions existing at
different times, and by the supposition associated with very different circumstances.
The one from having been co-existent with
certain circumstances has a power by the
law of association of exciting the recollection of those circumstances whenever it is
itself recollected: the other has the same
power over that particular combination of
circumstances with which it was associated,
merely because they were so impressed together on the mind at the same moment of
time. To say therefore that a particular
property of an object has a power of exciting the ideas of several other properties
of another object, of which it never made
a part, on the principle of association, is a
contradiction in terms. It's being essentially or comparatively the same with another property which did actually make part
of such an object no more proves the con-

sequences which fairly result from the principle of association than it would follow
from my looking at the same object at
which another has been looking, that I
must forthwith be impressed with all the
ideas, feelings and imaginations which have
been passing in his mind at the time.   This
last observation has been objected to on the
ground that there is no connection whatever between one man's ideas, and another's.   No doubt : but then it follows as
clearly (and that is all I meant to shew)
that the abstract identity of the objects or
impressions does not of itself produce this
connection, so that the perception of the
one must needs bring along with it the associated ideas belonging to the other.   The
objects or ideas are the same in both cases,
if that were all : but this is not sufficient
to prove that they must have the same ac-
companiments, or associations, because in
the one case they are impressed on different minds, and in the other on the same
mind at different times, which is expressly

contrary to the principle of association, unless we assume by the help of a verbal sophism that the same generical idea is the
same associated idea, and this again would
lead to the absurd consequence above
stated. It is not here necessary to give a
regular definition or account of what in
general constitutes sameness, or to inquire
whether strictly speaking such a relation
can ever be said to subsist between any two
assignable objects. Such an inquiry would
be quite foreign to the purpose, and I wish
to avoid as much as possible all useless
common-place subtleties, all such as whichever way they are determined can make no
alteration in the state of the argument. It
is plain in the present instance for example
that when it is stated that a particular idea
having been once associated with given circumstances, the *same* idea will ever afterwards excite the recollection of those circumstances, all that is meant is that the idea
in the latter case must be a *production*, con-
tinuation, or properly a recollection of

the former one, so as to retain the impression of the accidental modifications by which that idea was originally affected. It must be so far the same as to bear the same relation to the surrounding ideas, as to depend for what it is on what it has been, and connect the present with the past. It must be the old idea lurking in the mind with all it's old associations hanging about it, and not an entirely new impression with entirely new associations. This idea must therefore be originally derived from an individual impression in contradistinction to half a dozen different ones possessing the same absolute properties: for the whole point turns upon this, that such and such ideas have not naturally any sort of connection with certain other ideas, but that any one of these ideas having been actually associated with any of the others, this accidental relation begets a peculiar and artificial connection between them which is continued along with the remembrance of the ideas themselves.

Mr. Mac-Intosh, I remember, explained this principle in his lectures in the following manner. If, says he, any gentleman who has heard me in this place to-day should by chance pass by this way to-morrow, the sight of Lincoln's-Inn Hall will upon the principle we are now examining bring along with it, the recollection of some of the persons he has met with the day before, perhaps of some of the reasonings which I have the honour to deliver to this audience, or in short any of those concomitant circumstances with which the sight of Lincoln's-Inn Hall has been previously associated in his mind. This is a correct verbal statement, but it is liable to be misunderstood. Mr. Mac-Intosh is no doubt a man of a very clear understanding, of an imposing elocution, a very able disputant, and a very metaphysical lawyer, but by no means a profound metaphysician, not quite a Berkeley in subtlety of distinction. I will try as well as I am able to help him out in his ex-

planation. It is clear that the visible
image of Lincoln's-Inn Hall which any
one has presented to his senses at any given
moment of time cannot have been *previously* associated with other images and perceptions. Neither is a renewed sensible
impression of a particular object the same
with or in any manner related to a former
recollected impression of the same object
except from the resemblance of the one to
the other. There can be no doubt then
of the connection between my idea or recollection of Lincoln's-Inn Hall yesterday,
and the associated ideas of the persons
whom I saw there, or the things which I
heard, the question is how do I get this
idea of yesterday's impression from seeing
Lincoln's-Inn Hall to-day. The difficulty
I say is not in connecting the links in the
chain of previously associated ideas, but
in arriving at the first link,—in passing
from a present sensation to the recollection
of a past object. Now this can never be
by an act of association, because it is self-

evident that the present can never have been previously associated with the past. Every beginning of a series of associations, that is every departure from the continued beaten track of old impressions or ideas remembered in regular succession therefore implies and must be accounted for from some act of the mind which does not depend on association.

Association is an habitual relation between continuations of the same ideas which act upon one another in a certain manner simply because the original impressions were excited together. Let A B C represent any associated impressions. Let *a b c* be the ideas left in the mind by these impressions, and then let A M N represent a repetition of A in conjunction with a different set of objects. Now *a* the idea of A when excited will excite *b c* or the ideas of B C by association, but A as part of the sensible impression A M N cannot excite *b c* by association, because it has never been associated with B C, because it is not, like *a*, the production of the former impression A, but an entirely new impression made from without, totally unconnected with the first. I understand then from the nature of association how *a* will excite *bc*, but not how A excites *a*. I understand how my thinking of Lincoln's-Inn Hall, the impression of yesterday, should also lead me to think of other things connected with that impression according to the principle of association : but I cannot see how, according to this principle, there is any more connection between my seeing Lincoln's-Inn Hall to-day, and recollecting my having seen it yesterday than there is between the palace of St. Cloud, and the hovel in which Jack Shepherd hid himself when he escaped out of Newgate. Certainly the new impression is not the old one, nor the idea of the old one. What is it then that when this second impression is made on the mind determines it to connect itself with the first more than with any other indifferent impression, what carries it forward in that particular direction which is necessary to it's finding out it's fellow, or setting aside this geographical reasoning, what is there in the action of the one on the mind that necessarily revives that of the other? All this has clearly nothing to do with association.

A question however occurs here which perplexes the subject a good deal, and which I shall state and answer as concisely as I can. I have hitherto endeavoured to shew that a particular present impression cannot excite the recollection of a past impression by association, that is, that ideas cannot be said to excite one another by association which have never been associated. But still it may be asked whether a present impression may not excite the ideas associated with any similar impression, without first exciting a distinct recollection of the similar impression with which they were associated. Now, however we may reconcile it with the foregoing reasoning, it is certainly a fact that it does do so.

And I conceive it will not be difficult to account for this, according to the explanation above hinted at of the principle of association : for we may in general suppose any similar state of mind to be favourable to the readmission, or recollection of the ideas already associated *with* such a state of mind, whether the similarity is produced by a revival of the old idea, or by the recurrence of a similar external object. In this case however we must suppose that association is only a particular and accidental effect of some more general principle, not the sole-moving spring in all combinations which take place between our ideas: and still more, that similarity itself must be directly a very strong source of connection between them, since it extends beyond the similar ideas themselves to any ideas associated with them. On the other hand according to the Hartleian theory of association as carried on by the connection of different local impressions, which alone makes it

difficult to admit similarity as a distinct
source of connection between our ideas,
I am utterly unable to conceive how this
effect can ever take place, that is, I contend that there must be in this case a direct
communication between the new impression, and the similar old one before there
can be any possible reason for the revival
of the *associated* ideas, and then the same
difficulty will return as before, why one
similar impression should have a natural
tendency to excite another, which tendency cannot be accounted for from association, for it goes before it, and on this
hypothesis is absolutely necessary to account for it.——Whatever relates to local
connection must be confined to the individual impression and cannot possibly
extend to the class or *genus*. Suppose association to depend on the actual juxtaposition of two, or more local impressions
which being thus accidentally brought together have thrown a sort of grappling irons
over one another, and continue to act in

concert in consequence of this immediate local communication. It is clear that in this case none but the individual, or numerical impressions so united can have any power over each other. No matter how like any other impression may be to any of the associated ones,—if it does not agree in place as well as kind, it might as well not exist at all ; it's influence can no more be felt in the seat of the first, than if it were parcel of another intellect, or floated in the regions of the moon. Again suppose association to consist not in connecting different local impressions, but in reconciling different heterogeneous actions of the same thinking principle, "in sub-"duing the one even to the very quality "of the other," here the disposition of the mind being the chief thing concerned, not only those very identical impressions will coalesce together which have been previously associated, but any other very similar impressions to these will have a facility in exciting one another, that is in acting

upon the mind at the same time, their association depending solely on the habitual
disposition of the mind to receive such
and such impressions when preoccupied
by certain others, their local relation to
each other being the same in all cases.——
The moment it is admitted not to be necessary to association that the very individual impressions should be actually re-
vived, the foundation of all the inferences
which have been built on this principle
is completely done away.

Association is then only one of the ways
in which ideas are recollected or brought
back into the mind. Another view of the
subject remains which is to consider their
effects after they get there as well as how
they are introduced, why certain ideas
affect the mind differently from others,
and by what means we are enabled to
form comparisons and draw inferences.

If association were every thing, and the
cause of every thing, there could be no
comparison of one idea with another, no

reasoning, no abstraction, no regular con-
trivance, no wisdom, no general sense
of right and wrong, no sympathy, no foresight of any thing, in short nothing that
is essential, or honourable to the human
mind would be left to it. Accordingly
the abettors of this theory have set themselves to shew, that *judgment*, *imagination*,
&c. are mere words that really signify nothing but certain associations of ideas following one another in the same mechanical order in which they were originally impressed, and that all our feelings, tastes, habits and actions spring from the same
source. As I know of no proof whatever
that has, or can be given of either of these
paradoxes but that many of our opinions
are prejudices, and that many of our feel-
lings arise from habit, I shall state as concisely as I can my reasons for thinking that
association alone does not account either
for the proper operations of the understanding, or for our moral feelings, and
voluntary actions, or that there are other

general, original, independent faculties
equally necessary and more important in
the "building up of the human mind."
In every comparison made by the mind of
one idea with another, that is perception
of agreement, or disagreement, or of any
kind of relation between them, I conceive
that there is something implied which is
essentially different from any association
of ideas. Before I proceed, however, I
must repeat that in this question I stand
merely on the defensive. I have no positive inferences to make, nor any novelties
to bring forward, and I have only to defend
a common-sense feeling against the refinements of a false philosophy. I understand by association of ideas the recollecting or perceiving any two or more ideas
together, or immediately one after the
other. Now it is contended that this immediate succession, coexistence or juxtaposition of our ideas is all that can be
meant by their comparison. It is therefore a question in this case what becomes of

o

the ideas of likeness, equality, &c. for if there is no other connection between our ideas than what arises from positive association, it seems to follow that all objects seen, or if you please thought of together must be equally like, and that the likeness is completely done away by separating the objects or supposing them to be separated. As these ideas are some of the clearest and most important we have, it may be reasonably demanded that any attempt to account for them by resolving them into other ideas with which they have not at first sight the least connection should be perfectly clear and satisfactory. Let us see how far this has been done. It has been contended then that the only idea of equality which the mind can possibly have is the recollection of the *sensible impression* made by the meeting of the contiguous points, or ends of two strait lines for example*. Here two questions will arise. The

* See Essays by T. Cooper of Manchester. This very curious analysis was also delivered with great

first is whether the idea of equality is merely
a particular way of considering contiguity.
Secondly, whether association, that is the
succession or juxtaposition of our ideas can
ever of itself produce the idea of this relation between them. My first object will
be to inquire whether the perception of the
equality of two lines is the same with the
perception of the contiguity of their extremities, whether the one idea necessarily
includes every thing that is contained in
the other.

I see two points touch one another, or

gravity by Mr. Mac-Intosh to the metaphysical
students of Lincoln's-Inn. I confess I like ingenu-
ity, however misapplied, if it is but a man's own:
but the dull, affected, pompous repetition of nonsense is not to be endured with patience. In retail-
ing what is not our own, the only merit must be in the
choice, or judgment. A man, however, without ori-
ginality may yet have common sense and common
honesty. To be a hawker of worn-out paradoxes,
and a pander to sophistry denotes indeed a desperate
ambition.

that there is no sensible interval between them. What possible connection is there between this idea, and that of their being the boundaries of two lines of equal length? It is only by drawing out those points to a certain distance that I get the idea of any lines at all; they must be drawn out to the same distance before they can be equal; and I can have no idea of their being equal without dividing that equal distance into two distinct parts or lines, both of which I must consider at the same time as contained with the same limits. If the ideas merely succeeded one another, or even co-existed as distinct images, they would still be perfectly unconnected with each other, each being absolutely contained within itself, and there being no common act of attention to both to unite them together. Now the question is whether this perception of the equality of these two lines is not properly an idea of comparison, (in the sense in which

every one uses and feels these words)
which idea cannot possibly be expressed or
defined by any other relation between our
ideas, or whether it is only a round-about
way of getting at the old idea of the coincidence of their points or ends, which certainly is not an idea of comparison, or of
the relation between equal quantities simply because there are no quantities to be
compared. The one relates to the agreement of the things themselves one with
another, the other to their local situation.
There is no proving any farther that these
ideas are different, but by appealing to
every man's own breast. If any one should
choose to assert that two and two make six,
or that the sun is the moon, I can only
answer by saying that these ideas as they
exist in my mind are totally different. In
like manner I am conscious of certain operations in my own mind in comparing two
equal lines together essentially different
from the perception of the contiguity of
their extremities, and I therefore conclude

that the ideas of equality and contiguity
are not the same.

The second question is whether the idea
of contiguity itself is an idea of mere association, that is whether it is nothing more
than the recollection of a compound sensation. If by sensation is to be understood
the direct impression of the parts of any
outward object on corresponding parts of
an extended living substance, by which
means the general mass is converted from a
dead into a living thing, and that this is
the only difference that takes place, then
I deny that this combination of living
atoms, this diffusion of animal sensibility,
however exquisite or thrilling to the slightest touch, will ever give the idea of *relation*
of any kind whether of contiguity, coexistence, or any thing else either immediately at the time or by recollection afterwards. It has been said that *to feel is to
think,* " *sentir est penser.*" I believe that
this is true of the human mind, because the
human mind is a thinking principle, it is

natural to it to think, it cannot feel *with-out* thinking : but this maxim would not be at all true of such a human mind as is described by these philosophers, which would be equally incapable both of thought, and feeling as it exists in us. As this distinction is very difficult to be expressed, I hope I may be allowed to express it in the best way that I am able. Suppose a number of animalculæ as a heap of mites in a rotten cheese lying as close together as they can stick, (though the example should be of something " more drossy and divisible," of something less reasonable, approaching nearer to pure sensation than we can conceive of any creature that exercises the functions of the meanest instinct.) No one will contend that in this heap of living matter there is any idea of the number, position, or intricate involutions of that little, lively, restless tribe. This idea is evidently not contained in any of the parts separately, nor is it contained in all of them put together. That is, the aggregate of many actual sensations is, we here plainly see, a totally different thing from the collective idea, comprehension, or *consciousness* of those sensations as many things, or of any of their relations to each other. We may go on multiplying and combining sensations to the end of time without ever advancing one step in the other process, or producing one single thought. But in what I would ask does this supposition differ from that of many distinct particles of matter, full of animation, tumbling about, and pressing against each other in the same brain, except that we make use of this brain as a common medium to unite their different desultory actions in the same general principle of thought, or consciousness? Therefore if there is no power in this principle but to repeat the old story of sensation over again, if the mind is but a sort of inner room where the images of external things like pictures in a gallery are lodged safe, and dry out of the reach of the turbulence of the senses, but remaining as distinct from, and if I may so say as perfectly unknown to one another as the pictures on a wall, there being no general faculty to overlook and give notice of their several impressions, this medium is without any use, the hypothesis is so far an incumbrance, not an advantage. To perceive the relation of one thing to another it is not only necessary that the ideas of the things themselves should co-exist (which would signify nothing) but that they should be perceived to co-exist by the same conscious understanding, or that their different actions should be felt at the same instant by the same being in the strictest sense. If I am asked if I conceive clearly how this is possible, I answer no :—perhaps no one ever will, or can. But I do understand clearly, that the other supposition is an absurdity, and can never be reconciled with the nature of thought, or consciousness, of that power of which I have an absolute certainty in my own mind. If any one who still doubts of this will give me a satisfactory reason why he denies the same consciousness to different minds, or thinks it necessary to circumscribe this principle within the limits of the same brain but upon the supposition that one brain is one power, in some sort modifying and reacting upon all the ideas contained in it, I shall then be ready to give up my dull, cloudy, English mysticism for the clear sky of French metaphysics. Till then it is in vain to tell me that the mind thinks by sensations, that it then thinks most emphatically, then only truly when by decompounding it's essence it comes at last to reflect the naked impression of material objects. It is easy to make a bold assertion, and just as easy to deny it; and I do not know that there is any authority yet established by which I am bound to yield an implicit assent to every extravagant opinion which some man of celebrity has been hardy enough to adopt, and make others believe. It does not surely follow that a thing is to be disbelieved, the moment any one thinks proper to deny it, merely because it has been generally believed, as if truth were one entire paradox, and singularity the only claim to authority *.

* This subject of consciousness, the most abstruse, the most important of all others, the most filled with seeming inexplicable contradictions, that which bids the completest defiance to the matter-of-fact philosophy and can only be developed by the patient soliciting of a man's own spirit has been accordingly passed over by the herd of philosophers from Locke downwards. There is a short note about it in Hartley in which he flatly denies the possibility of any such thing. Lest what I have already said should therefore be insufficient to fix the attention of the reader on a subject which he may think quite exploded, I will add the account which Rousseau has given of the same subject, whose authority does not weigh the less with me because it is unsupported by the Logic of Condillac, or the book De l'Esprit.

" Me voici déjà tout aussi sûr de l'existence de l'univers, que de la mienne. Ensuite je réfléchis sur les objets de mes sensations, et trouvant en moi la faculté de les comparer, je me sens doué d'une force active que je ne savois pas avoir auparavant.

" Appercevoir, c'est sentir ; comparer, c'est juger .

I never could make much of the subject
of real relations in nature. But in whatever

juger et sentir ne sont pas la même chose. Par la
sensation, les objets s'offrent à moi séparés, isolés,
tels qu'ils sont dans la Nature ; par la comparaison,
je les remue, je les transporte, pour ainsi dire, je
les pose l'un sur l'autre, pour prononcer sur leur dif-
férence ou sur leur similitude, et généralement sur tous
leurs rapports. Selon moi, la faculté distinctive de
l'être actif, ou intelligent est de pouvoir donner un
sens a ce mot, *est*. Je cherche en vain dans l'être
purement sensitif cette force intelligente, qui super-
pose, et puis qui prononce ; je ne la saurois voir
dans sa nature. Cet être passif sentira chaque objet
séparément, ou même il sentira l'objet total formé
des deux, mais n'ayant aucune force pour les replier
l'un sur l'autre, il ne les comparera jamais, il ne les
jugera point.

" Voir deux objets à la fois, n'est pas voir leurs
rapports, ni juger de leurs différences ; appercevoir
plusieurs objets les uns hors des autres, n'est pas les
nombrer. Je puis avoir au même instant l'idée d'un
grand bâton et d'un petit bâton sans les comparer,
sans juger que l'un est plus petit que l'autre, comme
je puis voir à la fois ma main entière sans faire le
compte de mes doigts. Ces idées comparatives,
*plus grand*, *plus petit*, de même que les idées nu é-
riques d'*un*, de *deux*, &c. ne sont certainement pas

way we determine with respect to them,
whether they are absolutely true in nature,

des sensations, quoique mon esprit ne les produise,
qu'à l'occasion de mes sensations.

" On nous dit que l'être sensitif distingue les sensations les unes des autres par les différences qu'ont
entr'elles ces mêmes sensations : ceci demande ex-
plication. Quand les sensations sont différentes,
l'être sensitif les distingue par leurs différences :
quand elles sont semblables, il les distingue parce
qu'il sent les unes hors des autres. Autrement,
comment dans une sensation simultanée distingue-
roit-il deux objets égaux ? Il faudroit nécessaire-
ment qu'il confondît ces deux objets, et les prît
pour le même, sur-tout dans un système où l'on
prétend que les sensations représentatives de l'éten-
due ne sont point étendues.

" Quand les deux sensations à comparer sont apper-
cues, leur impression est faite, chaque objet est
senti, les deux sont sentis ; mais leur rapport n'est
pas senti pour cela. Si le jugement de ce rapport n'é-
toit qu'une sensation, & me venoit uniquement de
l'objet, mes jugemens ne me tromperoient jamais,
puisqu'il n'est jamais faux que je sente ce que je
sens.

" Pourquoi donc est-ce que je me trompe sur le rapport de ces deux bâtons, sur-tout s'ils ne sont pas

or are only the creatures of the mind, they
cannot exist in nature after the same man-

parallèles ? Pourquoi, dis-je, par exemple, que le
petit bâton est le tiers du grand, tandis qu'il n'en
est que le quart ? Pourquoi l'image, qui est la
sensation, n'est-elle pas conforme à son modele, qui
est l'objet ? C'est que je suis actif quand je juge,
que l'operation qui compare est fautive, et que mon
entendement, qui juge les rapports, mele ses erreurs
à la vérité des sensations qui ne montrent que les
objets.

Ajoutez à cela une réflexion qui vous frappera, je
m'assure, quand vous y aurez pensé ; c'est que si
nous étions purement passifs dans l'usage de nos sens,
il n'y auroit entr'eux aucun communication ; il nous
auroit impossible de connoître que le corps que nous
touchons, et l'objet que nous voyons sont le meme.
Ou nous ne sentirions jamais rien hors de nous, ou il
y auroit pour nous cinq substances sensibles, dont
nous n'aurions nul moyen d'appercevoir l'identité.

" Qu'on donne tel ou tel nom à cette force de mon
esprit qui rapproche et compare mes sensations ;
qu'on l'appelle attention, méditation, réflexion, ou
comme on voudra ; toujours est-il vrai qu'elle est
en moi et non dans les choses, que c'est moi seul qui
la produis, quoique je ne la produise qu'à l'occasion de l'impression que font sur moi les objets,

ner that they exist in the human mind. The forms of things in nature are manifold; they only become one by being united in the same common principle of thought. The relations of the things themselves as they exist separately and by themselves must therefore be very different from their relations as perceived by the mind where they have an immediate communication with each other. The things themselves can only have the same relation to each other that the ideas of things have in different minds, or that our sensible impressions must have to one another before we refer them to some inward conscious principle. Without this connection between our ideas in the mind there could be no preference of one thing

Sans etre maître de sentir ou de ne pas sentir, je le suis d'examiner plus ou moins ce que je sens.

Je ne suis donc pas simplement un être sensitif et passif, mais un être actif et intelligent, et quoi qu'en dise la philosophie, j'oserai prétendre à l'honneur de penser, &c.''—Emile, beginning of the third, or end of the second volume.

to another, no choice of means to ends, that is, no voluntary action. Suppose the ideas or impressions of any two objects to be perfectly distinct and vivid, suppose them moreover to be mechanically *associated* together in my mind, and that they bear in fact just the same proportion to each other that the objects do in nature, that the one is attended with just so much more pleasure than the other, and is so much more desirable, what effect can this of itself have but to produce a proportionable degree of unthinking complacency in the different feelings belonging to each, and a proportionable degree of vehemence in the blind impulse, by which I am attached to each of them separately and for the moment ? If there is no perception of the relation between different feelings, no proper comparison of the one with the other, there may indeed be a stronger impulse towards the one than there is towards the other in the different seats of perception which they severally affect, but there can be no reasonable attachment, no preference of

the one to the other in the same *general*
principle of thought and action. And
consequently on this supposition if the
objects or feelings are incompatible with
each other, I, or rather the different sensible beings within me will be drawn different ways, each according to it's own particular bias, blindly persisting in it's own
choice without ever thinking of any other
interest than it's own, or being in the least
affected by any idea of the general good
of the whole sentient being, which would
be a thing utterly incomprehensible.—To
perceive relations,—if not to choose between good and evil, to prefer a greater
good to a less, a lasting to a transient enjoyment belongs only to one mind, or spirit, the mind that is in man, which is the
centre in which all his thoughts meet, and
the master-spring by which all his actions
are governed. Every thing is one in nature,
and governed by an absolute impulse.
The mind of man alone is relative to other
things, it represents not itself but many

P

things existing out of itself, it does not therefore represent the truth by being sensible of one thing but many things (for nature, it's object, is manifold) and though the things themselves as they really exist cannot go out of themselves into other things, or compromise their natures, there is no reason why the mind which is merely representative should be confined to any one of them more than to any other, and a perfect understanding should comprehend them all as they are all contained in nature, or *in all*. No one object or idea therefore ought to impel the mind for it's own sake but as it is relative to other things, nor is a motive true or natural in reference to the human mind merely because it exists, unless we at the same suppose it to be stronger than all others.

But to return. I conceive first that volition necessarily implies thought or foresight, that is, that it is not accounted for from mere association. All voluntary action implies a view to consequences, a perception of the analogy between certain actions already given, and the particular action then to be employed, also a knowledge of the connection between certain actions and the effects to be produced by them; and lastly, a faculty of combining all these with particular circumstances so as to be able to judge how far they are likely to impede or assist the accomplishment of our purposes, in what manner it may be necessary to vary our exertions according to the nature of the case, whether a greater or less degree of force is required to produce the effect, &c. Without this " discourse of reason," this circumspection and comparison, it seems to be as impossible for the human mind to pursue any regular object as it would be for a man hemmed in on all sides by the walls of houses and blind alleys to see his way clearly before him from one end of London to the other, or to go in a strait line from Westminster to Wapping. One would think it would be sufficient to state the question in order to shew that mere association or the mechanical re-currence of any old impressions in a certain order, which can never exactly correspond with the given circumstances, would never satisfactorily account (without the aid of some other faculty) for the complexity and subtle windings and perpetual changes in the motives of human action. On the hypothesis here spoken of, I could have no comprehensive idea of things to check any immediate, passing impulse, nor should I be able to make any inference with respect to the consequences of my actions whenever there was the least alteration in the circumstances in which I must act. If however this general statement does not convince those who are unwilling to be convinced on the subject, I hope the nature of the objection will be made sufficiently clear in the course of the argument.

Secondly, it is necessary to volition that we should suppose the imaginary or general ideas of things to be efficient causes of action. It is implied in the theory we are

combating that some sort of ideas are efficient motives to action, because association
itself consists of ideas. Habit can be nothing but the impulsive force of certain
physical impressions surviving in their
ideas, and producing the same effects as
the original impressions themselves. Why
then should we refuse to admit the same,
or a similar power in any ideas of the same
kind, because they have been combined by
the imagination with different circumstances, or because a great many different ideas
have gone to make up one general feeling?
Why, if the inherent qualities of the ideas
are not changed, should not the effects
which depend on those qualities be the
same also? It cannot be pretended that
there is something in the nature of all
ideas which renders them inadequate to the
production of muscular action, the one
being a mental, the other a physical essence. For ideas are evidently the instruments of association, and must therefore
one way or other be the efficient causes of

voluntary action. The ideas of imagination and reason must be analogous to those of memory and association, or they could not represent their several objects, which is absurd.—It is to be remembered that the tendency of any ideas to produce action cannot be ascribed in the first instance to the accidental association between the original impression and some particular action, for the action is an immediate and natural consequence of the impression, and would equally follow from the same impression in any other circumstances, and ought to follow from any other idea partaking of the same general nature and properties. The proper effects of association can only apply to those cases, where an impression or idea by being associated with another has acquired a power of exciting actions to which it was itself perfectly indifferent. But this power cannot always be transferred from one impression to another, for there must be some original impression which

has an inherent independent power to produce action.

I do not know how far the rules of phi-
losophizing laid down by Sir Isaac New-
ton apply to the question, but it appears
to me an evident conclusion of common
sense not to seek for a remote and indirect
cause of any effect where there is a direct
and obvious one. Whenever therefore a
particular action follows a given impression,
if there is nothing in the impression itself
incompatible with such an effect, it seems
an absurdity to go about to deduce that action from some other impression, which has
no more right to it's production than that
which is immediately and obviously connected with it. In general it may be laid
down as a principle of all sound reasoning
that where there are many things actually
existing which may be assigned as the causes
of several known effects, it is best to di-
vide those effects among them, not arbitra-
rily to lay the whole weight of a complicated series of effects on the shoulders of

some one of them, generally singled out for no other reason than because it is the most remote and therefore the least probable. For this there can be no more reason than for supposing when I see a large building standing on a number of pillars, that the whole of it is secretly upheld by some main pillar in the centre, and that all the other pillars stand there for shew, not use. The principle that the fewest causes possible are to be admitted is certainly not true in the abstract; and the injudicious application of it has I think been productive of a great deal of false reasoning. Unquestionably, where there is no appearance of the existence of certain causes, they are to be admitted with caution : we are not fancifully to multiply them *ad libitum* merely because we are not satisfied with those that do appear, much less are we to multiply them gratuitously, without any reason at all. But where the supposed causes actually exist, where they are known to exist, and have an obvious connection with certain effects,

why deprive any of these causes of the real
activity which they seem to possess to make
some one of them reel and stagger under
a weight of consequences which nature never meant to lay upon it? This
mistaken notion of simplicity has been
the general fault of all system-makers,
who are so wholly taken up with some
favourite hypothesis or principle, that they
make that the sole hinge on which every
thing else turns, and forget that there is
any other power really at work in the
universe, all other causes being set aside
as false and nugatory, or else resolved
into that one.—There is another principle
which has a deep foundation in nature
that has also served to strengthen the same
feeling, which is, that things never act
alone, that almost every effect that can be
mentioned is a compound result of a series
of causes modifying one another, and that
the true cause of any thing is therefore
seldom to be looked for on the surface, or
in the first distinct agent that presents it-

self. This principle consistently followed
up does not however lead to the supposition that the immediate and natural causes
of things are nothing, but that the most
trifling and remote are something, it proves
that the accumulated weight of a long succession of real, efficient causes is generally
far greater than that of any one of them separately, not that the operation of the
whole series is in itself null and void but
as the efficacy of the first sensible cause is
transmitted downwards by association
through the whole chain. Association
has been assumed as the leading principle
in the operations of the human mind, and
then made the only one, forgetting first
that nature must be the foundation of every
artificial principle, and secondly that with
respect to the result, even where association has had the greatest influence, habit
is at best but a half-worker with nature, for
in proportion as the habit becomes inveterate, we must suppose a greater number

of actual impressions to have concurred in producing it.*

Association may relate only to feelings, habit implies action, a disposition to do something. Let us suppose then that it were possible to account in this way for all those affections which relate to old objects, and ideas, which depend on recalling past feelings by looking back into our memories. But the moment you introduce action (if it is any thing more than an involuntary repetition of certain motions without either end or object, a mere trick, and absense of mind) this principle can be of no use without the aid of some other faculty to enable us to apply old associated feelings to new circumstances, and to give the will a new direction.

Mr. Mac-Intosh in his public lectures used to deny the existence of such a feeling as general benevolence or humanity, on the ground that all our affections necessa-

* I here speak of association as distinct from imagination or the effects of novelty.

rily owe their rise to particular previous associations, and that they cannot exist at all unless they have been excited before in the same manner by the same objects. If I were disposed to enter particularly into this question, I might say in the first place that such a feeling as general benevolence or kindness to persons whom we have never seen or heard of before does exist. I should not scruple to charge any one who should deny this with the *mala fides*, with prevaricating either to himself, or others. It is a maxim which these gentlemen seem to be unacquainted with that it is necessary to strain an hypothesis to make it fit the facts, not to deny the facts because they do not square with the hypothesis. It generally happens, that, when a metaphysical paradox is first started, it is thought sufficient by a vague and plausible explanation to reconcile it tolerably well with known facts: afterwards it is found to be a shorter way and savours more of a certain agreeable daring in matters of philosophy

and dashes the spirit of opposition sooner
to deny the facts on the strength of the
hypothesis.—Independently however of
all experimental proof, the reasoning as it
is applied confutes itself. It is said that
habit is necessary to produce affection.
Now suppose this, in what sense is the
principle true? If the persons, feelings
and actions must be exactly and literally
the same in both cases, there can be no such
thing as habit: the same objects and circumstances that influenced me to-day cannot possibly influence me to-morrow. Take
the example of a child to whose welfare
the attention of the parent is constantly
directed. The simple wants of the child
are never exactly the same in themselves,
the accidental circumstances with which
they are combined are necessarily varying
every moment, nor are the sentiments and
temper of the father less liable to constant and imperceptible fluctuations. These
subtle changes, however, and this dissimi-
larity in subordinate circumstances do nor

prevent the father's affection for the child from becoming an inveterate habit. If therefore it is merely an extraordinary degree of resemblance in the objects which produces an extraordinary degree of strength in the habitual affection, a more remote and imperfect resemblance in the objects ought to produce proportionable effects. For example, the cries of a stranger's child in want of food are similar to those of his own when hungry, the expressions of their countenances are similar, it is also certain that wholesome food will produce similar effects upon both, &c. I am not here inquiring into the degree of interest which the mind will feel for an entire stranger (though that question was well answered long ago by the story of the Samaritan.) My object is to shew that as to mere theory there is no essential difference between the two cases; that a *continued* habit of kindness to the same person implies the same power in the mind as a general disposition to feel for others in the same situation;

and that the attempt to reason us out of a sense of right and wrong and make men believe that they can only feel for themselves, or their immediate connections is not only an indecent but a very bungling piece of sophistry.——The child's being personally the same has nothing to do with the question. The idea of personal identity is a perfectly generical and abstract idea, altogether distinct from association. Any other artificial, and general connection between our ideas (as that of the same species) might as well pass for association.

The commentators on Hartley have either not studied or not understood him. Otherwise his system could not have been supposed to favour the doctrine of selfishness. My quarrel with it is not that it proves any thing against the notion of disinterestedness, but that it proves nothing. He supposes that the human mind is neither naturally selfish, nor naturally benevolent; that we are equally indifferent to our own future happiness or that of others,

and equally capable of becoming interested
in either according to circumstances. [See
his account of the origin of self-love, page
370.] The difference between this account, and the one I have endeavoured to
defend is that I suppose that the idea of
any particular positive known good either
relating to ourselves or others is in itself an
efficient motive to action, whereas accor-
ing to Hartley no idea either of our own
interest or that of others has the least tendency to produce any such effect except
from association. He infers that there is
no essential, original desire of happiness
in the human mind, because this desire
varies according to circumstances, or is
different in different persons, and in the
same person at different times according
to the humour he is in, &c. This objection indeed holds true if applied to the
desire of happiness as a general indefinite
unknown object, that is, to a necessary,
mechanical, uniform disposition in man as
a metaphysical agent to the pursuit of good

as an abstract essence without any regard to the manner in which it is impressed on his imagination, to the knowledge which he can possibly have of any object as good, or to his immediate disposition to be affected by it. I have however all along contended that the desire of happiness is natural to the mind only in consequence of the idea, or knowledge of it, in the same manner that it is natural to the eye to see when the object is presented to it; to which it is no objection that this organ is endued with different degrees of sharpness in different persons, or that we sometimes see better than at others. Neither can I conceive how the associated impulses, spoken of in the passage above referred to, without an inherent, independent power in the ideas of certain objects to modify the will, and in the will to influence our actions can ever in any instance whatever account for voluntary action. I need not attempt to shew that the mechanical impulses to the pursuit of our own good or that of any

Q

other person derived from past associations
cannot be supposed to correspond exactly
and uniformly with the particular successive situations, in which it is necessary for
us to act, often with a view to a great number of circumstances, and for very complex ends. To suppose that the mechanical tendencies impressed on the muscles
by any particular series of past objects
can only require to be unfolded to produce
regular and consistent action is like supposing that a hand-organ may be set to
play a voluntary, or that the same types will
serve without any alteration to print a co-
lumn of a newspaper and a page of Tristram
Shandy. A child for instance in going
into a strange house soon after he had
learned to walk would not be able to go
from one room to another from the mere
force of habit, that is from yielding to, or
rather being blindly carried forward by the
impulse of his past associations with respect
to walking when at home. He would
run against the doors, get entangled among

the chairs, fall over the stair case : he would commit more blunders with his eyes wide open than he would otherwise do blind-folded. He would be worse off without his understanding than without his sight. He might feel his way without his eyes, but without his understanding neither his hands nor eyes would be of any use to him. He would be incorrigible to falls and bruises. Whoever has seen a blind horse stagger against a wall and then start back from it awkward and affrighted, may have some idea of the surprise which we should constantly feel at the effects of our own actions, but not of the obstinate stupidity with which we should persist in them.

To this it is replied, that the account here given does not include all the associ-ations which really take place : that the associations are general as well as particular, that there is the association of the general idea of a *purpose*, of the words *to walk*, *to go forwards*, &c. and that these general

associated ideas, and the feelings connected
with them are sufficient to carry the child
forward to the place he has in view according to it's particular situation. Association they say does not imply that the very
same mechanical motions should be again
excited in the same order in which they
were originally excited, for that long trains
of active associations may be transferred
from one object to another from the accidental coincidence of a single circumstance,
from a vague abstraction, from a mere
name. This principle does not therefore
resemble a book, but an alphabet, the
loose chords from which the hand of a
master draws their accustomed sounds in
what order he pleases, not the machinery
by which an instrument is made to play
whole tunes of itself in a set order.

I have no objection to make to this account of association but that nothing will
follow from it, and that nothing is explained by it. Let us see how it will affect the question in dispute.——We will

therefore return once more to the case of the child learning to walk. How then does this explanation account for his not running against any object which stands in his way in the pursuit of a favourite plaything, if he has not been used to meet with the same interruption before? Why does he not go strait on in the old direction in which he has always followed it?—Because he is afraid of the blow, which would be the consequence of his doing so, and he therefore goes out of his way to avoid it. This supposes that he has met with blows before, though not in running after his ball, nor from that particular object which he dreads, nor from one situated in the same way, or connected with the same associations. But this difference is of no importance according to the gloss: for it is not necessary that his fear or the effort which it leads him to make should proceed from the recollection of a former blow recurring in it's proper place, and stopping him by mechanical sympathy, as it had

actually done before, in the midst of his
career. He is stopped by the idea of a
pain which he has not yet felt, and which
can only affect him as a general, or representative idea of pain, the object being
new, and there being nothing in his past
associations in the order in which they are
recalled by memory to produce the necessary action. Here then he evidently *con-
structs* an artificial idea of pain beyond his
actual experience, or he takes the old idea
of pain which subsisted in his memory, and
connects it by that act of the mind which
we call imagination with an entirely new
object; and thus torn out of it's place in
the lists of memory, not strengthened by
it's connection with any old associated
ideas, nor moving on with the routine of
habitual impulses, it does not fail on that
account to influence the will and through
that the motions of the body.——Now if
any one chooses to consider this as the effect of association, he is at liberty to do so.
The same kind of association, however,

must apply to the interest we take in the feelings of others, though perfect strangers to us, as well as to the interest we feel for ourselves. All that can ever take place in the imaginary anticipation either of our own feelings or those of others can be nothing more than some sort of transposition and modification of the old ideas of memory, or if there is any thing peculiar to this act of the mind, it is equally necessary to our feeling any interest in our own future impressions, or those of others. According to this account therefore the old idea of physical pain must be called up whenever I see any other person in the like danger, and the associated action along with it, just as much as if I were exposed to the same danger myself. This is I believe the doctrine of sympathy advanced by Adam Smith in his " Theory of Moral Sentiments." It is in fact neither self-love nor benevolence, neither fear nor compassion, nor voluntary attachment to any thing, but an unmeaning game of battledore and shuttle-cock kept up between the nerves and muscles. But it seems to me a much more rational way to suppose that the idea does not lose it's efficacy by being combined with different circumstances, that it retains the same general nature as the original impression, that it therefore gives a new and immediate impulse to the mind, and that it's tendency to produce action is not entirely owing to the association between the original impression, and a particular action, which it mechanically excites over again. First, because the connection between the impression and action was not accidental but necessary, and therefore the connection between the idea and action is not to be attributed to association, but to the general nature of the human mind by which similar effects follow from similar causes. Secondly, if the imaginary or general idea were entirely powerless in itself except as a means of exciting some former impulse connected with physical pain, none but the very identical action formerly excited could

result from it, that is if I could not avoid
an object in the same way that I had formerly
done I should not attempt to avoid it at
all, but remain quite helpless. Thirdly,
because the ideas of future objects having
no effect at all on my feelings or actions,
and the connection between the original
associated impressions being the strongest
and most certain of all others, any particular train of mechanical impulses being
once set in motion would necessarily go on
in the old way unrestrained by any idea of
consequences till they were stopped again
by actual pain.——It is plain however that
the activity of the understanding pre-
vents this rough rebuke of experience, that
the will (and our actions with it) bends and
turns and winds according to every change
of circumstances and impulse of imagination, that we need only foresee certain evils
as the consequences of our actions in order
to avoid them. The supposition that the
idea of any particular motion necessary to
a given end or of the different motions

which combined together constitute some
regular action is sufficient to prodnce that
action by a subtle law of association can
only apply to those different motions after they are willed, not to the willing them.
That is, there must be a previous determi-
nation of the will, or feeling of remote
good connected with the idea of the action
before it can have any effect.   The idea of
any action must be in itself perfectly indifferent, being always advantageous, useless,
or mischievous according to circumstances.
I cannot therefore  see any reason according to  this  hypothesis  why I should will
or be  inclined to make  any exertions  not
originating  in  some  mechanical  impulse
that happens to  be  strongest  at the time,
merely because  they may  be  necessary to
avoid an imaginary evil which of itself does
not cause the slightest emotion in my mind:
on the contrary, if the barely thinking of
any external action is  always immediately
to  be  followed by that action  without a
particular warrant from the  will,  there

could be no such thing as reasonable action among men, our actions would be
more ridiculous than those of a monkey,
or of a man possessed with St. Vitus's
dance; they would resemble the diseased
starts and fits of a madman, not the actions
of a reasonable being. We should thrust
our hands into the fire, dash our heads
against the wall, leap down precipices, and
commit more absurdities every moment of
our lives than were performed by Don
Quixote with so much labour and study
by way of penance in the heart of the
Brown Mountain. The *momentum* of the
will is necessary to give direction and con-
stancy to any of our actions; and this
again can only be determined by the ideas
of future good and evil, and the connection which the mind perceives between certain actions, and the attainment of the one
or the prevention of the other. If our actions did not naturally slide into this track,
if they did not follow the direction of reason wherever it points the way, they must

fall back again at every step into the old
routine of blind mechanical impulse, and
headlong associations that neither hear, nor
see, nor understand any thing.—Lastly the
terms *general association* mean nothing of
themselves. I have done a particular action with a certain purpose, or I have had
in my mind at the time the general idea of
a purpose, of something useful connected
with my action. What has this to do with
my ability to perform any other action, be
it ever so different, because it is also connected with a purpose? The associated
idea either of a particular purpose, or of
a purpose generally speaking can only have
an immediate tendency to excite that particular action, with which it was associated,
not any action whatever, merely because it
may have a connection with some remote
good. So of any number of actions. For
let ever so many different actions have been
associated with the idea of a purpose, this
will not in the least enable me to perform
any intermediate action, or to combine the

old actions in a different order with a view
to a particular purpose, unless we give to
the idea of this particular purpose as a
general idea of good an absolute power to
controul our actions, and force them into
their proper places. I grant indeed that
having once admitted a direct power in
ideas of the same general nature to affect
the will in the same manner we may by a
parity of reasoning suppose that this power
is capable of being transferred by association to the most indifferent ideas, which,
as far as they resemble one another, will
operate as general motives to action, or
give a necessary bias to the will. But if
this analogy holds with respect to secondary and artificial motives which are not in
their own nature allied to action, surely it
must hold much more with respect to the
direct, original motives themselves, the
ideas of good and evil, where the power
inheres in the very nature of the object.
My being led to perform different actions
with which the same abstract idea of utility

is connected is not therefore properly owing to association, but because any ideas
or motives of the same kind whether derived from a new impression, or made out
by the imagination, or only general feelings must naturally influence the will in
the same manner, and this impulse being
once given, the understanding makes choice
of such means as are perceived to be necessary to the attainment of the given object. For, after all, the execution of our
purposes must be left to the understanding.
The simple or direct ideas of things might
excite emotion, volition, or action; but
it would be the volition of the objects
or feelings themselves, not of the means
necessary to produce them. Feeling alone
is therefore insufficient to the production
of voluntary action. Neither is it to be
accounted for from association. The actual
means necessary to the production of a
given end are willed, not because those very
means have been already associated with
that particular end (for this does not hap-

pen once in a thousand times) but because those means are known to be inseparable from the attainment of that end in the given circumstances.

There is however another objection to the disinterested hypothesis, which was long ago stated by Hobbes, Rochefocault, and the author of the Fable of the Bees, and has been since adopted and glossed over by Helvetius. It is pretended that in wishing to relieve the distresses of others we only wish to remove the uneasiness which pity creates in our own minds, that all our actions are necessarily selfish, as they all arise from some feeling of pleasure or pain existing in the mind of the individual, and that whether we intend our own good or that of others, the immediate gratification connected with the idea of any object is the sole motive which determines us in the pursuit of it.

First, this objection does not at all affect the question in dispute. For if it is allowed that the idea of the pleasures or pains of others excites an immediate interest

in the mind, if we feel sorrow and anxiety
for their imaginary distresses exactly in the
same way that we do for our own, and are
impelled to action by the same motives,
whether the action has for it's object our
own good or that of others, the nature of
man as a voluntary agent must be the same,
the effect of the principle impelling him
must be the same, whether we call this
principle self-love, or benevolence, or
whatever refinements we may introduce
into our manner of explaining it. The relation of man to himself and others as a
moral being is plainly determined, for whether a regard to the future welfare of himself and others is the real, or only the os-
tensible motive of his actions, they all tend
to one or other of these objects, and to one
as directly as the other, which is the only
thing worth inquiring about. All that can
be meant by the most disinterested benevolence must be this immediate sympathy with
the feelings of others, and it could never
be supposed that man is more immediately

affected by the interests of others than he can be even by his own. If by self-love we understand any thing beyond the impulse of the present moment, it can be no more a mechanical thing than the most refined and comprehensive benevolence. I only contend then that we are naturally interested in the welfare of others in the same sense in which we are said to be interested in our own future welfare. Self-love used in the sense which the above objection implies must therefore mean something very different from an exclusive principle of deliberate, calculating selfishness, which must render us indifferent to every thing but own advantage, or from the love of physical pleasure and aversion to physical pain, which would produce no interest in any but sensible impressions *.

Supposing therefore that our most generous feelings and actions were equivocal, the object only bearing a shew of disinterestedness, the motive being always selfish,

R

this would be no reason for rejecting the common use of the term *disinterested bene-volence*, which expresses nothing more than an immediate reference of our actions to the good of others, as self-love expresses a conscious reference of them to our own good, as means to an end. This is the proper meaning of the terms. If there is any impropriety in the one, the other must be equally objectionable, the same fallacy lurks under both.

Secondly, the objection is not true in itself, that is, I see no reason for resolving the feelings of compassion, &c. into a principle of mechanical self-love. That the motive to action exists in the mind of the person who acts is what no one can deny. The passion excited and the impression producing it must necessarily affect the individual. There must always be some one to feel and act, or there could be no such thing as feeling or action *. It

* See preface to Butler's Sermons.

cannot therefore be implied as a condition in the love of others, that this love should not be *felt* by the person who loves them, for this would be to say that he must love them and not love them at the same time, which is palpable nonsense. This absurd inference, I say, could never be implied in the common use of the terms, as it could never be imagined that in order to feel for others, we must in reality feel nothing. This distinction proves clearly that it is always the individual who *loves*, but not that he always *loves himself;* for it is to be presumed that the word *self* has some meaning in it, and it would have absolutely none at all, if nothing more were intended by it than any object or impression existing in the mind. Self-love would merely signify the love of something, and the distinction between ourselves and others be quite confounded. It therefore becomes necessary to set limits to the meaning of the term.

First, it may signify, as explained above, the love or affection excited by the idea of our own good, and the conscious pursuit of it as a general, remote, ideal thing. In this sense, that is considered with respect to the proposed end of our actions, I have shewn sufficiently that there is no exclusive principle of self-love in the human mind which constantly impels us to pursue our own advantage and nothing but that, and that it must be equally absurd to consider either self-love or benevolence as a physical operation.

Another sense of the term may be, that the indulgence of certain affections necessarily tends without our thinking of it to our immediate gratification, and that the impulse to prolong a state of pleasure and put a stop to whatever gives the mind the least uneasiness is the real spring and overruling principle of our actions. No matter whether the impression existing in my mind is a sensation or an idea, whether it is an idea of my own good or that of another, it's effect on the mind is entirely owing to this involuntary attachment to

whatever contributes to my own gratification, and aversion from actual pain.
Or the mind is so constructed that without forethought or any reflection on itself
it has a natural tendency to prolong and
heighten a state of pleasurable feeling, and
instantly remove every painful feeling.
This tendency must be wholly unconscious;
the moment my own gratification is indirectly adverted to by the mind as the consequence of indulging certain feelings, and
so becomes a distinct motive to action, it
returns back into the limits of deliberate,
calculating selfishness; and it has been
shewn that there is nothing in the idea of
our own good which makes it a proper
motive of action more than that of others.
There appears to be as little propriety in
making the mechanical tendency to our
own good the foundation of human actions. In the first place, it may be sufficient to deny the mere matter of fact, that
such is the natural disposition of the human mind. We do not on every occasion

blindly consult the interest of the moment, there is no instinctive, unerring bias
to our own good, controuling all other
impulses, and guiding them to it's own
purposes. It is not true that in giving
way to the feelings either of sympathy or
rational self-interest (by one or other of
which feelings my actions are constantly
governed *) I always yield to that impulse
which is accompanied with most pleasure
at the time. It is true that I yield to the
strongest inclination, but not that my
strongest inclination is to pleasure. The

* As far as the love of good or happiness operates
as a general principle of action, it is in this way. I
have supposed this principle to be at the bottom of
all our actions, because I did not desire to enter
into the question. If I should ever finish the plan
which I have begun, I shall endeavour to shew that
the love of happiness even in the most general sense
does not account for the passions of men. The love
of truth, and the love of power are I think distinct
principles of action, and mix with, and modify all
our pursuits. See Butler as quoted above.

idea of the relief I may afford to a person
in extreme distress is not necessarily accompanied by a correspondent degree of
pleasurable sensation to counterbalance
the painful feeling his immediate distress
occasions in my mind.   It is certain that
sometimes the one and sometimes the other
may prevail without altering my purpose
in the least: I am held to my purpose
by the idea (which I cannot get rid of)
of what another suffers, and that is in my
power to alleviate his suffering, not that
that idea is always the most agreeable contemplation I could have.   The mind is
often haunted by painful images and recollections, not that we court their company,
but that we cannot shake them off, even
though we strive to do it.   Why does a
woman of the town always turn round to
look at another finer than herself? Why
does the envious man torment himself by
dwelling on the advantages of his rival?
Not from the pleasure it affords him. Why
then should it be maintained that the feel-

ings of compassion, generosity, &c. cannot possibly actuate the mind, but because
and in as far as they contribute to our
own satisfaction? Those who willingly perform the most painful duties of friendship
or humanity do not do this from the immediate gratification attending it; it is as
easy to turn away from a beggar as to relieve him; and if the mind were not
governed by a sense of truth, and of the
real consequences of it's actions, we should
treat the distresses of others with the same
sort of feeling as we go to see a tragedy because we know that the pleasure will be
greater than the pain. There is indeed
a false and bastard kind of feeling which
is governed altogether by a regard to this
reaction of pity on our own minds, and
which therefore serves more strongly to
distinguish the true. So there is a false
fear, as well as a refined self-interest. We
very often shrink from immediate pain,
though we know that it is necessary to our
obtaining some important object; and at

other times undergo the most painful operations in order to avoid some greater evil
at a distance.——In the sense which the objection implies, my love of another is not
the love of myself but as it operates to produce my own good. The mind is supposed
to be mechanically attached to, or to fly
from every idea or impression simply as it
affects it with pleasure, or pain. And if
this were the case, it might with some propriety be said to be actuated by a principle
of mechanical or practical self-love. If
however there is no such principle regu-
lating my attachment to others by my own
convenience, very little foundation will be
left for the mechanical theory. For, secondly,
the real question is, why do we sympathize
with others at all? It seems we are first
impelled by self-love to feel uneasiness at
the prospect of another's suffering, in order
that the same principle of tender concern
for ourselves may afterwards impel us to
get rid of that uneasiness by endeavouring
to prevent the suffering which is the cause

of it. It is absurd to say that in compassionating the distress of others we are only affected by our own pain or uneasiness, since this very pain arises from our compassion. It is putting the effect before the cause. Before I can be affected by my own pain, I must first be put in pain. If I am affected by, or feel pain and sorrow at an idea existing in my mind, which idea is neither pain itself nor an idea of my own pain, I wonder in what sense this can be called the love of myself. Again, I am equally at a loss to conceive how if the pain which this idea gives me does not impel me to get rid of it as it gives *me* pain or as it actually affects myself as a distinct, momentary impression, but as it is connected with other ideas, that is, is supposed to affect another, how I say this can be considered as the effect of self-love. The object, effort or struggle of the mind is not to remove the idea or immediate feeling of pain from the individual or to put a stop to that feeling as it affects his

temporary interest, but to produce a dis-
connection (whatever it may cost him) between certain ideas of other things existing in his mind, namely the idea of pain,
and the idea of another person. Self, mere
physical self, is entirely forgotten both
practically and consciously. My own
good is neither the exciting cause nor the
immediate result of the feeling by which I am
actuated. I do not shrink from the idea
of the pain which another feels as it affects
myself, but it excites repugnance, uneasiness, or active aversion in my mind as it
affects, or is connected with the idea of
another; and it is because I know that certain actions will prevent or remove that
pain from that other person according to
the manner in which I have perceived effects to be connected together in nature,
that I *will* those actions for that purpose,
or that their ideas take hold of my mind,
and affect it in such a manner as to produce their volition. In short, the change
which the mind endeavours to produce is

not in the relation of a certain painful idea
to itself as perceiving it, but in the relation
of certain ideas of external things to one another.   If this is not sufficient to make the
distinction intelligible, I cannot express
it any better.  " Oh, but" (it will be
said) " I cannot help feeling pain when I
see another in actual pain, or get rid of
the idea by any other means than by re-
lieving the person, and knowing that it
exists no longer." But will this prove
that my love of others is regulated by my
love of myself, or that my self-love is subservient to my love of others ?  What hin-
ders me from immediately removing the
painful idea from my mind but that my
sympathy with others stands in the way of
it ? That this independent attachment to
the good of others is a natural, unavoidable feeling of the human mind is what
I do not wish to deny.  It is also, if
you will, a mechanical feeling ; but then
it is neither a physical, nor a selfish mechanism.  I see colours, hear sounds,

feel heat, and cold, and believe that two
and two make four by a certain mechanism,
or from the necessary structure of the human mind; but it does not follow
that all this has any thing to do with self-
love.——One half of the process, namely
the connecting the sense of pain with
the idea of it, is evidently contrary to
self-love; nor do I see any more reason
for ascribing the uneasiness, or active impulse which follows to that principle,
since my own good is neither thought of
in it, nor does it follow from it except
indirectly, slowly and conditionally. The
mechanical tendency to my own ease or
gratification is so far from being the real
spring or natural motive of compassion
that it is constantly overruled and defeat-
ed by it. If it should be answered that
these restrictions and modifications of the
principle of self-love are a necessary consequence of the nature of a thinking being,
then I say that it is nonsense to talk of
mechanical self-love in connection with a

power of reflection, that is, a mind capable of perceiving the consequences of
things beyond itself, and of being affected
by them. To ask therefore whether if
it were possible to get rid of my own uneasiness without supposing the uneasiness
of another to be removed I should wish
to remove it, is foreign to the purpose;
for it is to suppose that the idea of another's uneasiness is not an immediate object of uneasiness to me, or that by making
a distinction of reflection between the idea
of what another suffers, and the uneasiness
it causes in me, the former will cease to
give me any uneasiness, which is a contradiction. A question might as well
be put whether if pleasure gave me
pain, and pain pleasure, I should not
like pain, and dislike pleasure. So long
as the idea of what another suffers is a necessary source of uneasiness to me, and
the motive and guide of my actions, it
is not true that my only concern is for
myself, or that I am governed solely by

a principle of self-interest.—The body has a mechanical tendency to shrink from physical pain: this may be called mechanical self-love, because, though the good of the individual is not the object of the action, it is the immediate and natural effect of it. The movement which is dictated by nature is directly followed by the cessation of the pain by which the individual was annoyed. The evil is completely removed with respect to the individual, the moment the object is at a distance from him; but it only exists as it affects the individual, it is therefore completely at an end when it ceases to affect him. The only thing necessary therefore is to produce this change in the relation of the body to the object; now this is the exact tendency of the impulse produced by bodily pain, that is, it shrinks *at* the pain and *from* the object. The being does not suffer a moment longer than he can help it: for there is nothing that should induce him to remain in pain. The body is not tied down to do penance under the discipline of external objects, till by fulfilling certain conditions, from which it reaps no benefit, it obtains a release; all it's exertions tend immediately to it's own relief. The body (at least according to the account here spoken of) is a machine so contrived, that, as far as depends on itself, it always tends to it's own good, in the mind, on the contrary, there are numberless lets and impediments that interfere with this object inseparable from it's very nature; the body strives to produce such alterations in it's relation to other things as conduce to it's own advantage, the mind seeks to alter the relations of other things to one another; the body *loves* it's own good, for it tends to it, the understanding is not governed solely by this principle, for it is constantly aiming at other objects. To make the two cases of physical uneasiness, and compassion parallel, it would be necessary to suppose either an involuntary tendency in the muscles to remove every

painful object from another through mechanical sympathy, or that the real object
of compassion was to remove the nervous
uneasiness, occasioned by the idea of another's pain, as an abstract sensation existing in my mind, totally unconnected with
the idea which gave rise to it.

Lastly, should any desperate metaphysician persist in affirming that my love of
others is still the love of myself because
the impression exciting my sympathy
must exist in my mind and so be a part of
myself, I should answer that this is
using words without affixing any distinct
meaning to them. The love or affection
excited by any general idea existing in my
mind can no more be said to be the love
of myself than the idea of another person
is the idea of myself because it is I who
perceive it. This method of reasoning,
however, will not go a great way to prove
the doctrine of an abstract principle of
self-interest, for by the same rule it would
follow that I hate myself in hating any

other person. Indeed upon this principle the whole structure of language is a
continued absurdity. Whatever can be
made the object of our thoughts must be
a part of ourselves, the whole world is
contained within us, I am no longer
John or James, but every one that I
know or can think of, I am the least part
of myself, my self-interest is extended as
far as my thoughts can reach, I can love
no one but I must love myself in him,
in hating others I also hate myself. In
this sense no one can so much as think of,
much less love any one besides himself,
for he can only think of his own thoughts.
If our generous feelings are thus to be
construed into selfishness, our malevolent
ones must at least be allowed to be disinterested, for they are directed against ourselves, that is against the *ideas* of certain
persons in our minds. If I can have no
feeling *for* any one but myself, I can have
no feeling *about* any one but myself. Suppose I am seized with a fit of rage against

a man, and take up a knife to stab him,
the quantity of malice, which according to
the common notion is here directed against
another, must according to this system
fall upon myself. I see a man sitting on
the opposite side of a table, towards whom
I think I feel the greatest rancour, but in
fact I only feel it against myself. For
what is this man whom I think I see before me but an object existing in my mind,
and therefore a part of myself? The
sword which I see is not a real sword, but
an image impressed on my mind; and
the mental blow which I strike with it is
not aimed at another being out of myself,
(for that is impossible) but at an idea of
my own, at the being whom I hate
within myself, at myself. If I am always
necessarily the object of my own thoughts
and actions, I must hate, love, serve, or
stab myself as it happens. It is pretended
by a violent assumption that benevolence
is only a desire to prolong the idea of
another's pleasure in one's own mind,

because that idea exists there: malevolence must therefore be a disposition to prolong the idea of pain in one's own mind for the same reason, that is, to injure one's-self, for by this philosophy no one can have a single idea which does not refer to, nor any impulse which does not originate in self.—If by self-love be meant nothing more than the attachment of the mind to any object or idea existing in it, or the connection between any object or idea producing affection and the state of mind produced by it, this is merely the common connection between cause and effect, and the love of every thing must be the love of myself, for the love of every thing must be the love of the object exciting it. On the contrary, if by self-love be meant my attachment to or interest in any object in consequence of it's affecting me personally or from the stronger and more immediate manner in which certain objects and impressions act upon me, then it cannot be affirmed without an absurdity that all affection whatever is self-love. So if I see a man wounded, and this sight occasions in me a painful feeling of sympathy, I do not in this case feel for myself, because between that idea or object impressed on my mind and the painful feeling which follows there is no such positive connection as there is between the infliction of the same wound on my own body ; and the physical pain which follows it. Will it be pretended by any one, on whose brain the intricacies of metaphysics have not had the same effect as the reading of romances had on the renowned knight of La Mancha, that a piece of wood which I see a man cutting in pieces, and so is an object existing in my mind, is a part of myself in the same sense as a leg or an arm ?  For my own part, as I am not at all affected by the hacking and hewing which this piece of wood receives, or all the blows with which it rings, which are to me mere harmless flourishes in the air, it seems to me a very different thing. The one idea is myself in a simple, very abstract sense indeed, the other idea is myself in the common emphatical sense, it is a reduplication or aggravation of the idea, the object becomes myself by a double right, I am sensible *in* the object as well as *to* it. I should say, then, that when the sight of another person wounded excites a feeling of compassion in my mind, this is not a selfish feeling in any narrow or degrading sense of the word, which is the only thing in dispute. (If selfishness is to mean generosity, there is an end at once of the dispute.) And that for this plain reason, that the connection between the visible impression and the feeling of pain is of a totally different kind from the connection between the feeling of pain, and the same wound when inflicted on my own body. The one is an affair of sensation, the other is entirely an affair of imagination. My love of others cannot therefore be built upon the love of myself, considering this last as the effect of " physical sensibility", and the moment we resolve self-love into the rational pursuit of a remote object, it has been shewn that the same reasoning applies to both, and that the love of others has the same necessary foundation in the human mind as the love of ourselves.

**THE END**

*Printed by E. Hemsted, New-street, Fetter-lane.*

## ERRATA.